A Poetic Odyssey

A Poetic Odyssey

RYAN DUTTON

RESOURCE *Publications* • Eugene, Oregon

A POETIC ODYSSEY

Copyright © 2024 Ryan Dutton. All rights reserved. Except for brief quotations in critical publications or reviews, no part of this book may be reproduced in any manner without prior written permission from the publisher. Write: Permissions, Wipf and Stock Publishers, 199 W. 8th Ave., Suite 3, Eugene, OR 97401.

Resource Publications
An Imprint of Wipf and Stock Publishers
199 W. 8th Ave., Suite 3
Eugene, OR 97401

www.wipfandstock.com

PAPERBACK ISBN: 979-8-3852-1166-1
HARDCOVER ISBN: 979-8-3852-1167-8
EBOOK ISBN: 979-8-3852-1168-5

VERSION NUMBER 02/28/24

Contents

Introduction | vii

Book I: Tales of Life

Inseparable Lovers | 3
Moonlight Sonata | 5
Colors of Rainbow | 7
Mozart's Prague | 8
Shah Jahan's Taj Mahal | 9
Dilruba | 10
Vysehrad Cemetery | 11
Time Flies | 13
In Search of Lost Time | 14
Proustian Moment | 15
Nostalgia | 17
My Grandpa | 18
Walking in the Self's
  Shadow | 19
Mirror of Your Soul | 20
Bill vs Bill | 21
Abdul the Thief | 22
A Trader's Tragedy | 23
A Lawyer's Remorse | 25
Dreams | 28
An Argentinian's Cry | 30
Determination | 31
Mount Everest | 32

Suffering | 34
Ahmed the Refugee | 35
Generations Past | 38
Slavery | 39
Children of Earth | 41
Earth's Lament | 42
Digital Drugs | 43
Psionic Corps | 45
My Blue Jeans | 47
Hunger | 49
Stop the Cycles | 50
Police Brutality | 51
Son of a Bitch | 52
To Be Kind or to Be Right | 54
Rape | 56
Love is Not for Sale | 57
A Zookeeper's Song | 58
Mumba | 59
Hank and His Rocky | 60
Jane and Aunt Becky | 62
Oh Tragedy! | 64
September 11th, My Final
  Moments | 65

v

Book II: Romantic Verses

Birth of Venus | 69
On the Walls of My
  Heart | 70
Sunset on the Vltava | 72
Scarlet Cloud | 74
Shrouded Moon | 75
Starry Night | 76
Astral City | 77
Oh Cloud | 79
Ich Liebe dich, I Love
  You | 81
Petrin Hill | 82
Autumn Melancholy | 83
Adieu | 84
My First Love | 85
Aline | 86
Lament of Orpheus | 87
Tantric Union | 88
Your Eyes | 89
Vicissitudes | 90
Non, Je Ne Regrette Rien, No
  Regret | 91
La Vie en Rose, Through
  Rose-Colored Glasses | 92
Solitude | 93
Adagio, Slowly | 94
My Twin Flame | 95
A Poet's Gift | 96

Book III: War

Ukraine War, a Reflection | 99
Blood | 100
War | 102
A Soldier's Adieu | 103
Letter from the Front
  Line | 104
The Scar | 106
Sophie's Choice | 107
Warship to Worship | 108
Om Shanti, Oh Peace! | 109

Book IV: Lights of Life

The Hand | 113
Divine Grace | 114
Faith | 115
Ocean of Life | 117
Sail on | 118
Author | 119
Confessions of Dr. Faust | 120
The Sacred Prophecy | 121
Stairway to Heaven | 122
Oh Judas | 123
The Battle Within | 125
Dedication | 126

God is Dead, Nietzsche is Not | 128
A Fakir and His Idol | 129
Creation of Adam | 130
Awakening to Oneness | 132
Doubt the Doubters! | 133
Resolve | 134
Social Acceptance | 135
Be Yourself | 136
Maya | 137
Ego | 138
Time the Jester | 139
Change of Wheels | 140
Your Higher Self | 142
The Universe Within | 143

Fetus | 145
Resilience | 146
Life | 147
Gratitude | 149
Blessings | 150
United through Him | 151
The Sacred Tongue | 152
Shiva's Dance | 153
Death | 155
A Divine Encounter | 156
The Train of Destiny | 157
Urn of Ashes | 160
On the Shore of Eternity | 162

Introduction

While composing my poetry, I have often found myself engaged in a sacred, silent dialogue that has emerged from the depths of time, a ceaseless dialogue between the human spirit and the cosmos, whispers that transcend time, culture, and limits of our finite understanding of life. I have felt inexplicably as if standing on the threshold between this visible world and that wondrous, ineffable, intangible one, as I try to articulate all those complex, profound currents of thoughts and emotions felt within my poetic experience. All these verses that I have worked on for over a decade which now appear in this book are not just for the simple pleasure of reading on an idle day, but rather it is like taking my readers into a spiritual and aesthetic realm where the human spirit meets the divine and beauty intertwines with the abstract and the imaginary.

Each verse in this collection is a fragment of my deepest thinking, my philosophy, and my worldview. Each one reveals a part of my inner sanctum, the realm of my emotions crafted by my life as a human. Poetry for me is a sacred endeavor, cultivation of both our intellect and passion, a pursuit that transcends the boundaries of culture, nationality, religion, or social status. It is an adventure of the artistic nature of our spirit, an attempt to weave the threads of our lives into a tapestry that reflects the universal essence of life.

Embedded in this tapestry of my poetry is my spiritual philosophy, the quest of the human spirit for transcendence, a journey into the mystic landscapes where the finite seek communion with the infinite, an interplay between the seen and the unseen, the known and the unknown. Spirituality, as I view it, is not confined to the rituals and doctrines of organized religions but is a pulsating heartbeat, a silent whisper that permeates the very essence of our existence. It is a voyage inward where the seeker unravels the layers of an overweening ego to discover the eternal, divine spark that connects us all.

Also, spirituality is not an escape from our worldly life, society, family, or friends into a sort of ascetic life where one spends one's days in a meditative state. Quite the contrary, spirituality is a unique way of engaging with them all, society, family, and friends. Spirituality is about understanding the true nature of humans as spiritual beings who have all gathered on this physical plane, the earth, for a unique physical experience. It is through my poetry that I have sought to express this spiritual engagement with our world, to capture poetically the timeless wisdom of the spiritual masters of our human civilization, and to embrace the universality of human experience.

If spirituality is a journey inward, humanism is the outward embrace of our shared experiences. It places the essence of humanity above any faith or religion. In a world often fraught with division and strife, I have sought to celebrate in my poetry the common threads that bind us all—the threads of love, compassion, kindness, forgiveness, and the shared pursuit of a more harmonious world.

My exploration of the meaning of life began during my adolescent years, a period marked by the inherent curiosity that defines youth. Thoughts echoed in my mind like ancient hymns seeking answers to questions like "Who are we beyond our physical form? Why do we exist? Where do we come from? And what is our destination after the death of our physical bodies?" Little did I realize that these questions were not mere intellectual pondering; they were the roots of a spiritual odyssey that would shape the very essence of my being in the years ahead.

I sought solace in the doctrines of spiritual scriptures, the teachings of Christ and Buddha, the Bhagavad Gita, and the mystic writings of visionaries like William Blake, Alan Watts, and Tagore. I was deeply touched by Victor Hugo, Goethe, Somerset Maugham, and Dostoevsky. Despite finding fragments of truth in the scriptures and the works of all those noble thinkers, a persistent sense of dissatisfaction lingered, a yearning for a deeper understanding of the cosmic fabric that we are all woven into, the meaning of this life on earth.

The saga of my spiritual journey took an unexpected turn when three extraordinary books serendipitously entered my life, transforming my convictions and subsequently altering my vision of life. Dr. Raymond Moody's "Life After Life," Dr. Brian Weiss's "Many Lives, Many Masters," and Robert Schwartz's "Your Soul's Plan" became the trinity of enlightenment that I never knew I was searching for. I felt this was a moment of epiphany, a watershed in my spiritual journey. I discovered a magic light that unveiled the mysteries that had eluded me for so long. The revelations in these books not only redefined for me the meaning of life but also shed new light on my perception of the teachings of the spiritual masters and the timeless wisdom imparted by the sages throughout the ages.

Dr. Raymond Moody's trailblazing work "Life After Life" takes us on a journey into the realm of near-death experiences (NDEs) and the profound insights they offer into the afterlife. Dr. Moody's meticulous cataloging of his patients' experiences reveals a consistent pattern of encounters with a bright light, a review of one's life, and a sense of peace and transcendence. These shared elements not only provide a compelling narrative of an existence beyond the physical realm but also align with similar accounts in various spiritual philosophies.

Drawing on Moody's insights, we begin to perceive life as a continuum, where the physical life is but one temporary chapter in the eternal journey of the soul; death is not an end but a transition—a doorway to another dimension of consciousness. This perspective dispels the fear and anxiety often associated with death, thus fostering a more enlightened and exalted view of the inevitable.

Dr. Brian Weiss's "Many Lives, Many Masters" takes us into the realm of past-life regression therapy, offering deep, revealing insights into the continuity of the soul across multiple lifetimes. The revelations in "Many Lives, Many Masters" contribute to a broader understanding of the soul's journey and the interconnectedness of those different lifetimes. Weiss's elaboration of the concept that we are spiritual beings having a series of human experiences corroborates the teachings of mystics and spiritual masters throughout history across many different cultures.

As we evolve through successive lifetimes, accumulating wisdom and lessons that transcend the boundaries of time, we gradually traverse the path of spiritual ascension which is the primary goal of this earthly life. This perspective disputes the notion of a singular, mortal existence, opening the door to a more expansive understanding of the purpose behind the intricacies of life.

In "Your Soul's Plan," Robert Schwartz takes us deeper into those intricacies of life, the purpose of the soul's journey on earth or the physical plane. Exploring the concept of pre-birth planning, Schwartz contends that we actively choose the circumstances and challenges of our earthly existence to facilitate spiritual growth and learning. This concept of pre-birth planning contradicts the conventional narrative of random and chaotic life events. Whether it be overcoming adversity, experiencing loss, or encountering challenges, each aspect of our earthly journey serves a purpose predetermined by our souls.

Schwartz's work is fundamental to the understanding that life's difficulties are not arbitrary punishments but opportunities for spiritual refinement. This perspective shifts the paradigm from being a victim to being empowered. This immediately prompts a reassessment of our understanding of suffering, emphasizing its transformative potential in the grand process of our spiritual evolution.

After discovering Moody, Weiss, and Schwartz, I was embraced by a new dawn of realization. The collective wisdom derived from this trinity of enlightenment converged into a harmonious philosophy that emphasizes love as the most fundamental spiritual force. This philosophy resonates with the divine message of Christ, the message of love, empathy, goodwill, and the interconnectedness of all beings. The teachings of Christ, as viewed through the lens of this spiritual synthesis, aligned with the idea that love and light are not just abstract concepts but the very fabric of existence, a universal tenet that transcends religious boundaries, echoing the core messages of unity and compassion found in many spiritual traditions.

While the works of Dr. Brian Weiss and Robert Schwartz are grounded in contemporary perspectives and experiences, the fundamental themes support the ancient wisdom found in the Upanishads, a collection of philosophical texts composed between 700 and 500 BCE, that explores the nature of reality, the self or Atman, and the supreme divine or Brahman. The Upanishads emphasize the cyclical nature of existence often referred to as reincarnation, a fundamental concept in Weiss's book, and the idea that the soul undergoes a continuous process of rebirth on the physical plane until it achieves liberation or moksha and reunites with the divine. Schwartz's work reinforces the idea of the law of Karma, another central element in the Upanishadic teachings, that explains how the actions in one's past life influence the circumstances and experiences in one's present life. As explained by Schwartz, the challenges an individual faces are not random but are chosen by the soul to fulfill karmic purposes. The Upanishads teach us the importance of self-realization and the recognition of the divine within oneself. The concept of Atman merging with Brahman is fundamental to the Upanishadic hermeneutics. In the same vein, Weiss and Schwartz's works highlight the transformative power of self-discovery, spiritual awareness, and ultimately spiritual ascension. While the sources and methodologies differ, the underlying tenets connect modern therapeutic approaches to ancient philosophical insights, illuminating the universality of these profound truths unveiled in different cultural milieus.

Interwoven with my spirituality, my poetry is also a celebration of my aesthetics, my perspective on beauty. Beauty, as I perceive it, is not superficial embellishment but an expression of the divine harmony that permeates the cosmos. Beauty is not meant for a simple pursuit of pleasure. The existence of the divine must be seen in its ordinary as well as its extraordinary form to reveal the beauty behind the veil of the material world. Along with the beauty visible in the natural world, I have tried to capture in my poetry the reflection of the inner beauty, the Elysian incandescence that resides in our souls.

Poetry, as I have felt, is inherently endowed with some form of transformative power. It can elevate the human spirit to transcend the limitations of the mundane and connect us with the sublime. The canvas of poetry has always been my sacred space, a place where I can paint with emotions to evoke the sublime. Poetry is not necessarily a passive medium for entertainment. To me, it has been an active engagement with the profound mysteries of our existence, a call to contemplation, an invitation to plumb the depths of our own consciousness, and an opportunity to connect with our shared human experiences. In poetry, we discover the universality of emotions, a timeless melody that binds us all.

At the heart of poetry's beauty lies its ability to encapsulate the essence of life in a few carefully chosen words. Unlike prose, which often explicates the theme, poetry condenses experiences, thoughts, and emotions into concise and potent verses. Moreover, poetry possesses the unique ability to convey complex emotions with unparalleled depth and resonance. Through metaphors, similes, and vivid imagery, poets can unveil the hidden facets of human feelings that often elude ordinary prose. Poetry's capacity to convey the inexpressible makes it a poignant and emotionally charged form of literature, rendering it beautiful and equally dramatic in its profound connection with the human heart.

In the vast spectrum of human civilization, poetry has often appeared to me as a silent sentinel, guarding the moral compass of societies through the ages. As we peruse some thought-provoking verses, we encounter not only the beauty of language but also the ethical undercurrents that run through each line and stanza. Poetry can inspire ethical reflection, stir our conscience, and bring about change. Through its verses, it can stimulate a dialogue on the ethical dimensions of our existence—the choices we make, the paths we tread, and the impact of our actions on the fabric of society. Like a beacon in the darkness, poetry illuminates the often-shadowy recesses of our ethical deliberations, urging us to reflect upon the moral imperatives that shape a just and compassionate society.

As I discovered the transformative power of poetry, its elegance as a form of literature, and its footprints in both the aesthetic and ethical dimensions of our lives, my affinity for poetry burgeoned over the years, and my spiritual odyssey slowly merged with my poetic odyssey. The collection of the verses in this book is a reflection of that magnificent convergence. The verses, emanating from the cornucopia of my personal experiences and introspection, are arranged in four distinct, evocative sections: Tales of Life, Romantic Verses, War, and Lights of Life. Each section unfolds as a narrative fabric, weaving together the threads of my thoughts, emotions, passions, and contemplation.

Life, with all its intricacies and nuances, unfolds in myriad tales in the first section, "Tales of life." Here, poetry becomes a mirror reflecting the human experiences—joyous celebrations, poignant sorrows, the intoxicating magic of love, the shadows of jealousy, the tendrils of insecurity, the tears of the oppressed, and the heart-wrenching tragedies that shape our existence. These verses delve into the heart of what it means to be a human, inviting readers to explore the depths of their own emotions and the shared reservoir of humanity. In this section, poetry acts as a conduit that carries the expression of our collective memories, providing solace and understanding in the face of life's unpredictable journey. Whether celebrating the triumphs of the human spirit or mourning the losses that leave indelible marks on our souls, these tales of life are an ode to the resilience inherent in human nature.

In my poetic odyssey, "Romantic Verses" emerge as a delicate dance of the heart, expressing the ineffable beauty of love and the complex emotions that accompany it. This section not only encompasses traditional expressions of romanticism but also explores the broader theme of the romantic spirit—an ethos that has prevailed across different cultural and temporal contexts. The verses within this section serve as whispers of passion, declarations of devotion, and reflections on the transformative power of love. Here, I have navigated the terrain of the heart, marking the delicate balance between ecstasy and heartbreak, trying to create a lyrical symphony that resonates with the universal language of love.

Amidst the beauty of our existence, the shadows of conflict appear and the specter of war looms over our Mother Earth. The poems in the section "War" carry a poignant message about the horrific nature of war and its profound impact on humanity. Through a poetic voice that yearns for peace, these verses bear witness to the collective scars etched on the human soul by the ravages of war. While exploring the darkness of conflict, I have tried not only to condemn the atrocities but also to illuminate the path toward reconciliation and understanding. War, as a theme, has been a stage for the expression of empathy, a plea for harmony, and a reminder of the shared responsibility to strive for a world free from the shackles of violence.

The final section "Lights of Life" ascends to a spiritual and philosophical plane. The verses here resonate with the themes of Christian philosophy, humanism, death, reincarnation, karma, and the mysteries that transcend our mortal understanding. The poems here are contemplative, offering glimpses of enlightenment and urging readers to delve into the realms of introspection and spiritual awakening. As lights piercing through the darkness, these verses serve as beacons and explore the metaphysical aspects of our existence. They draw upon the wisdom of the ages, inviting readers to reflect on some of the profound questions that have reverberated in the caverns of human thought for centuries.

In the conclusion of this modest preface, let me express my deepest gratitude to all my readers for embarking on this poetic odyssey with me. It is an honor to share these verses with them, to offer them a glimpse into the realms of my thoughts, emotions, and most importantly my creative spirit. The act of reading is not a solitary endeavor but a communion between the author and the reader, an experience that should transcend many differences we may have.

Should my readers credit me with any originality, I would consider them guilty of excessive fondness for my writing. None of the ideas contained in my poetry are mine. I have bathed in the streams of wisdom and exalted thoughts of countless philosophers, mystics, and divinely inspired writers who have enlightened us for thousands of years. As a poet, I am a humble messenger, a carrier of sacred tidings of the universe. Let us all continue with our unending quest for the meaning of life, appreciation of divine beauty, and understanding of this vast tapestry of our existence.

Ryan Dutton
January 2024

BOOK I

Tales of Life

Inseparable Lovers

Bill, on death row, stood with fate unjust,
Accused falsely, awaiting the lethal thrust.
Despite the monstrous fate, a sliver of relief,
Beloved Beth's visit, comforting his grief.
Their love blazed softly, yet pained their souls,
Separation's weight, as darkness unfolds.
For Beth, a steady job, a lifeline's thread,
Still, her man, Bill, was filled with dread.

August 15th, of irony, there was no dearth,
Wife's birthday, their last meeting on earth.
Etched in hearts, this bittersweet snare,
Love clung tightly, death's sinister stare.
Each moment precious, as time flew past,
In shadow's grip, their love steadfast.
Bill, unjustly accused, on fate's lonely lane,
Still, there was love on life's grave pane.

In a special room, on August's somber eve,
Beth visited Bill, for whom she'd grieve.
Cake and wine shared, their hearts were bound.
In each other's care, some solace was found.
But as the hour came, when they must part,
Beth stood with teardrops, breaking Bill's heart.
Bill, with a hug, held Beth very tight.
Oh Gosh, a razor emerged; what a dreadful sight!

Whoosh! with a flourish, a horrifying act,
Beth's throat sliced open, a moment so exact.
Agony and screams choked the cold air,
Bill's tears mixed with anguish, a love's despair.
"I love you," he cried, "We'll be together forever."
"To make me live, a chance, this will be never!"
In the tragic chaos that was left behind,
It was love twisted, shattered, forever defined.

Moonlight Sonata

When Nature brings her wondrous play,
She intertwines her path and finds her way
Into our world, into our soul,
Lays it all out as if in a silver bowl.
In Night's veil, in a mood sublime,
In pensive thoughts, it's a poet's time.
Sitting in my study with wine in my hand,
It's now time to go to an ethereal land.
With Moonlight Sonata, the serenade, I begin—
A perfect melody to open the soul within.

Looking out the window I catch a view,
Revealing a sight, both old and new—
Sweet Moon, a silver orb so bright,
With her radiant presence in the ebony night.
As if on cue, the stars appear,
And gilded bees around her so clear.
Nature and music, divinely intertwined,
A cosmic symphony, subtle and refined—
Moonlight Sonata, a serenade rare,
Echoes of the past now fill the air.

Well, I could have suffered a soldier's plight,
With a rotting wound in Ukraine's night.
I could have been that man, homeless and lost,
Maybe a harlot selling her soul to pay her cost,
A sick man in a slum, plagued by despair,
Or a poor cripple bound to a wheelchair.
With empathy, my heart does weep
For wretched souls in agony steep.
Moonlight Sonata, a balm for my sorrow,
With each fleeting day, I can live for tomorrow.

Colors of Rainbow

On a cold afternoon, I stroll with delight
Across Charles Bridge that looks so bright.
A voice melodious captures my ear;
I turn to behold, a blind woman I hear.
In a soprano's voice, she sings Ave Maria.
It pierces my heart like a poignant aria.

Transported to another world, I stand in awe.
Thoughts and emotions flood like a waterfall's draw.
What a melody from the dark!
A captive angel with the voice of a lark.
She, who's never seen colors, paints rainbows in the air,
With charm and mystique that's just so rare.

The old bridge whispers secrets, as harmonies unfold.
I stand frozen in time, in the melody's hold.
But my mobile interrupts, awakening my state—
My wife's voice reminds me, dinner can't wait.
Salmon, mashed potatoes, cherry tomatoes to savor,
A touch of wine would make the evening braver.

With tears in my eyes, I leave a heartfelt gift—
A stovka in her box gently left to drift.
Terrestrial pain forgotten, ethereal joy found,
Immersed in a moment that'll forever me astound.

Mozart's Prague

In Mozart's Prague, late eighteenth century,
Art and culture thrived, a vibrant reverie.
A spirit of creativity filled the air,
Melodies weaved an exotic affair.
Breathtaking architecture, medieval smells,
Gothic splendor and ringing church bells.
Enchanted by Mozart's mesmerizing tune,
Prague's heart thrummed under a silver moon.

Exquisite Josefina, her spirit would ignite
Romantic flames, passion's secret light.
From Don Giovanni's tales, passion set ablaze,
To requiem's mournful choir, a haunting phrase,
From St. Nicholas to the theater's stage,
Mozart's music echoed on history's page.
In Prague's air, an ethereal charm would rise,
Mozart's melodies, a gift from the skies.

The spirit of Mozart, forever intertwined,
With Prague's golden spirit, majestic, refined,
Timeless symphonies, their bond profound,
A love affair on music's hallowed ground.
We'll forever celebrate this magic connection,
Mozart's Prague, a place for joyous reflection,
Where melodies bloomed, and souls were set free,
In the heart of Prague, Mozart's legacy.

Shah Jahan's Taj Mahal

From a lover's grief, a monument did rise,
Taj Mahal's story, Love's eternal ties.
The mausoleum, built on Love's hallowed ground,
By emperor Shah Jahan, in his sorrow profound.

Oh Shah Jahan, as Time's streams gently flow,
Life, youth, and riches, they come, and they go.
Yet in your heart, you longed to immortalize grief,
For the time left on your throne would be brief.

Your voice soared, filling the heavens' heart,
Seducing Time with beauty, like a magic art.
You immortalized Death with your wonder,
Capturing tears in stone's eternal slumber.

The jewels of your throne are scattered by Time's tide,
But Taj Mahal remains, a tear's glistening pride,
A testament to Love, crafted by a hand divine,
A pearl in Time's hand, an immortal shrine.

Dilruba

In the palace of the Ottoman's imperial reign,
A beauty bound in the harem's gilded chain,
A slave of elegance in this captive life,
Whose spirit soars through harmony and strife,
The charming eyes and secrets in their gleam,
In the harem's labyrinth, she'd often dream;
Enslaved by Fate, yet in her spirit, free,
A woman named Dilruba, a mystery as we see.
Silken veils shroud her graceful form,
In the sultan's palace, where luxuries swarm;
Yet beneath the jewels, a fire burns,
A glowing heart, for freedom it yearns.
She tends to the roses by the garden's keep,
Into their petals, her dreams would often seep.
Each blossom whispers of a world afar,
Where freedom glimmers like a distant star.
Dilruba, an unsung name in history's verse,
A ravishing slave in this life diverse,
Into the sultan's heart, she finds her way,
Still, in her secret dreams, she'd always sway.

Vysehrad Cemetery

In twilight's shadow, I wander through the place,
Where headstones stand like sentinels in space.
Each epitaph, a glimpse of the past,
A tribute to life, in love's mold cast.

I feel the gravity of history's hold,
As I trace my steps, strange moods unfold.
A sepulchral realm and I feel I'm not alone,
The spirits of the departed must have flown.

Some of the headstones catch my eyes;
Death and departure, their beauty defies.
The enchantment of this melancholy scene,
A timeless art where sorrow's hues convene.

The trees, like guardians, watch over all;
Their rustling leaves in whispers seem to call
A lullaby to those who lie in rest,
A peaceful melody, their spirits' bequest.

Among the blooms of love and fond farewell,
I walk and contemplate this somber spell.
It's a dance, of life and death in unity,
An ode to what was, and what yet will be.

In Vysehrad cemetery, serene and sacred,
There's a sense of oneness that is created,
Melded with the realm of art and lore,
I feel connected with those who lived before.

Time Flies

On Time's wings, as moments swiftly flee,
In ceaseless flight, a Life's decree,
Ephemeral whispers echo in the air;
For Life's transient beauty, we must care.
Each passing moment, a gem precious,
Of which, we ought to be conscious.
Stop and behold the blessings that we find
In every fleeting moment, a treasure to bind,
For in this dance of Time, we must embrace
The transient nature of life's ardent chase.

In Search of Lost Time

In the labyrinth of my memory's trace,
Where time's elusive threads interlace,
So many treasures in the moments lost,
In Proustian realms, my mind's embossed.
A madeleine's taste, a fleeting view,
Unlocks the door to memories anew,
In the cup of tea, the scent of lime,
A journey through the corridors of time.
Like a cork adrift in the vast sea,
My soul in search of what life used to be,
The past, a portrait in shadows and light,
In search of lost time, a ceaseless flight.
In reverie, I dip my mind's quill,
In the inkwell of remembrance, still,
To pen the verses of an ordinary life,
Its joys and triumphs, its trials and strife.
Memories are the mirrors that I find
Reflecting truths of the heart and mind.
In this Proustian reflection, I can see
The wonders and fragility of life's tapestry.

Proustian Moment

On a summer day, accidentally I tread,
Republic Square, where festivity is spread.
Flags of vibrant hues dance in the air,
Drums' rhythmic beats echo with care.
Incense and flowers perfume the breeze,
Tropical fruits' aroma, a delightful tease.
A grand chariot bedecked with grace,
Beckons all to partake in this joyous chase,
Hare Krishna's Ratha Yatra, what a sight!
In the heart of Prague, festive and bright.
With a mango lassi, my chosen delight,
I settle on a bench, distanced from the sight.
Then, a wondrous occurrence, I witness here,
The festival's aroma and the lassi, Oh dear!
They awaken a version of me, a distant hue,
My past self resurfaces like morning dew.
A floodgate of emotions opens deep within,
And childhood memories are revived therein.
A time traveler, to a distant realm I'm borne,
In Calcutta's labyrinthine lanes, reborn.
At dusk, scents of oil lamps and jasmine's grace,
A little chariot I pull, with glee on my face.
The flute's melody in the breeze does soar,
Grandpa, grandma, uncle, and aunt, I adore.
Though earthly planes they no longer hold,
Their presence lingers and slowly unfolds.

As reveries embrace my wandering mind,
Teddy nuzzles my hand for a lucky find.
Whimpering, he seeks treats, a joyful plea,
Awakening me from my dream, a love's decree.
In memory's gentle hug, past and present blend,
Revived by love's warmth, my soul transcends.

Nostalgia

With an adventure each day, a treasure to explore,
In an open playground on imagination's shore,
We enjoyed a simple joy on a summer day,
And sang a melody in an evening play.
Beneath a tree, secrets were shared,
Friendships woven and compared.
In Imagination's kingdom, there was no end,
Built castles in the sand, laughed with a friend.
In innocence's shadow, time stood still,
As laughter rang out, with voices so shrill!
Thoughts of those wonders, so pure and wild,
We're in a child's heart, a universe undefined.

My Grandpa

At my tender age, just eleven years past,
Grandpa departed, a man in a saint's mold cast.
His presence still lingers, etched upon my soul,
A canvas of memories that life doesn't control.

With my eyes shut, I still see a picture so clear—
A vivid portrait held closely and very dear.
Grandpa's face, bathed in a divine glow,
On death's lap, an ethereal aura was bestowed.

That illumination, a reflection of realms unknown,
Through death's gateway, a saintly journey shown.
Not darkness, but a world of radiant bliss,
Where a saint finds a home, an eternal kiss.

Temples and churches, I rarely attend.
Yet in my heart's sanctum, a sacred blend,
An altar reserved, forever it shall be,
For Grandpa's spirit, in love's sanctuary.

Walking in the Self's Shadow

The shadow, born from unspoken desires,
A mirror image of your inner fires,
A creature lurking in the abyss of your mind,
Unseen, yet ever present, it does bind.
The shadow knows your hidden fears,
Unveiling truths through forbidden tears.
It speaks in whispers, haunting and low,
Revealing parts that you fear to show.

Embrace the shadow as part of your soul.
With self-compassion, let healing unfold.
In mindful meditation, find solace and peace,
A dialogue with the unconscious, let it release.
Understand your nature, your beliefs, your core,
Let reasons guide you, as you seek to explore
A richer, fuller life, where shadows fade away;
Embrace the light, and let it lead the way.

Mirror of Your Soul

The mirror of your soul reveals depths within,
Virgin realms of the self, where shadows spin.
With an open heart, wander through your core,
In a voyage of self-reflection, you learn to explore.
In moments quiet, heed the echoes of your heart,
Embracing every aspect, the broken and the smart.
In shadows cast, find the light to lead the way,
Let awareness bloom, with every passing day.

Recognize the patterns, the triggers, the fears,
A dance of understanding that dried your inner tears.
In humble grace, see the power that you possess,
Your real worth, you gradually learn to assess.
Know your true self, let your purpose come alive,
The seeds of transformation in the depths of self-thrive.
With gratitude and reverence, embrace the journey's art,
Self-reflection and awareness to brighten your heart.

Bill vs Bill

In a world of words, Bill Wallace thrived,
A journalist renowned, his story arrived.
One fateful day, he unearthed a secret forbidden,
Senator Bill Boyd's affair that was carefully hidden.
Months dragged on, the story grew bold,
A vendetta it seemed, as the truth he'd unfold.
Personal grudges, now tangled and intertwined,
Wallace's motives obscure, his ideas maligned.

Bill Boyd, ashamed, was forced to resign,
The scandal's weight too heavy a line.
Yet fate's irony soon took its stage,
As Wallace's own life turned a turbulent page.
Within months, a divorce case was in sight,
Wallace's wife filing suit, infidelity's blight.
Judgement revealed—shadows previously unknown,
Wallace's own darker self, truth was now shown.

In Wallace's own soul, a battle did brew,
Projected desires, his conscience askew.
Despising the Senator for his mirror's reflection,
Bill Wallace failed to grasp his inner imperfection.
The very enemy, named Bill, he fought outside
Was his own self, where darkness did reside.
His repressed urges, his shadow, a hidden decree,
It blinded his judgment, a truth he couldn't see.

Abdul the Thief

In a slum where dreams are few,
Lived Abdul, a boy with temper askew,
Capricious yet thoughtful, a mix so wild,
A soul of contrasts, a personality styled.
On an errand, at a hardware store, he was seen,
With watchful eyes, he looked very keen.
With a shopper's wallet, a theft unseen,
He slinked away like a shadow in between.

Restless, he returned to the spot of his mission,
Only to witness a boy accused merely on suspicion.
Abdul watched, helpless, as fury raged,
In the throes of violence, the boy was caged.
Back home, his stolen wallet, concealed,
Dreams of fortune, his heart had revealed.
But now stung by remorse, his spirit forlorn,
No words to speak, his dreams were torn.

Appetite vanished, a dinner small,
In night's darkness, an internal squall,
In bed he sobbed, his soul's shadows entwined,
Immersed in confused thoughts, a tortured mind.
A world of true dreams, where remorse would creep,
In solitude's embrace, his secrets to keep,
For young Abdul, it was a night of bitter tears,
A contrite soul, burdened by fears.

A Trader's Tragedy

> In this world there are only two tragedies:
> One is not getting what one wants,
> and the second is getting it.
> —Oscar Wilde

It's the capital market, a tale of greed,
A trader's heart with ambition's seed.
Bitcoin's rise, a boat to catch,
Fearing loss, he made the match.
Thrilled with dreams, he barely slept,
Visions of riches, his mind had kept.
New cars, vacations, oh what delight,
His heart danced with joy every night.

As profits grew, he held on tight,
Thinking more gains were in sight.
But fortune's favor began to fade,
The price started a downward cascade.
Still upbeat, he held his ground,
Thinking the price would soon rebound.
While profit halved, a hope he'd find,
To sell, he would still be disinclined.

Alas, the price dropped with greater force,
Back to where he had set his course.
Depressed, he clung to his hope's thread,
Refusing to believe he was misled.
Some days, a glimmer of hope would emerge,
As feelings surged to stir his urge.
But trends prevailed, with doom encased,
His joy turned to woe, his hopes displaced.

Below his purchase, it finally lay,
With hopes crushed, a disheartened display.
In a desperate state, he reached the brink,
Selling his bitcoin, he couldn't think.
Triumph turned to defeat's cruel jest,
His hope devoured by despair's unrest.
In a trading game, a lesson learned,
A loser's path, he had discerned.

A Lawyer's Remorse

In a small town in India,
On his veranda, Neil sat,
A brilliant attorney, somehow,
Distracted by this and that.
He had had a recent triumph,
A high-profile case won,
Yet, echoed in the community
Were tales of injustice done.
A man of wealth and power,
A malicious, wretched soul,
Escaped justice's grip,
After taking a life, his cruel toll.
A tribal man murdered
In a dispute so small,
This acquittal left the town
With a sad shadow's pall.

Life's ironies gnawed at Neil,
He felt the dilemma's weight,
But faithful to his profession,
His resolve wouldn't abate.
Virtuous in life, he believed,
He had sworn to defend
His clients, guilty or not,
His duties he had to attend.
Shockingly, as he was musing,

The tribal man's widow appeared,
With terror writ large on her gaze,
And by her rage her face seared.
Her raspy voice cursed Neil
In a savage, bitter tone,
He, speechless and shaken,
Slowly stood up to atone.

Yet resolute the woman stood,
Her primordial anger held tight,
Holding a knife in her hand,
Oh, what a frightening sight!
Surprisingly, from the shadow,
Johnny the shepherd sprang,
Fierce and Loyal Johnny, his fangs
On the woman's flesh rang.
Her scream echoed in the villa,
The servant rushed to the scene,
Neil gingerly grabbed the knife,
Oh Johnny, his courage so keen!
The police were called,
The woman restrained was led away,
Amidst the horrific chaos,
Neil's thoughts went astray.

Master of the law, debates, arguments,
But how helpless Neil felt,
Besieged by a guilty conscience,
Down his spirit knelt.
A conflict within his soul,
Heart and mind at odds,

As Neil gazed at the night,
The stars, the darkened gods.
Johnny's bravery had spared his life,
A friend, a hero to admire,
Yet, in the weight of his conscience,
There was a relentless fire.
In contemplative bewilderment,
Adrift he remained,
A brilliant attorney,
Tormented and pained.

Dreams

In the storm of struggles, adversity takes its toll,
You stand amidst a tempest, a steadfast, resolute soul.
When shadows cast their doubts, and voices despair,
Look deep within, your immortal strength lies in there.

The journey may be rugged, strewn with thorns and strife,
But it's your inner dialogue that shapes the course of life.
Believe in your spirit, its beauty, its power to endure,
For in your heart, the flames of dreams forever burn pure.

Ignore the detractors, who doubt your strength,
For your self-confidence will guide you at length.
With the power of will, you'll weather every storm,
As you tread the path, your dreams will take their form.

Success, it's often said, is born from pain and sweat,
But remember, friend, you haven't seen your limits yet.
With each setback and stumble, with every trial faced,
Your character is tempered, and your spirit embraced.

You hold the reins of fate in life's true art,
Each choice, each resolution, etched on your heart,
Embrace a challenge, as a chance to learn and grow,
With resilience, your armor, your dreams will surely flow.

With dreams in your eyes, let your heart's voice prevail,
You're the sculptor of your destiny in life's grand tale.
With unswerving faith, and a tireless zeal,
You'll craft a life, where all dreams are real.

An Argentinian's Cry

In jubilant streets, a nation unites,
A coveted trophy, gleaming under golden lights.
Argentina has triumphed, the World Cup is won,
A moment of euphoria, our dream is spun.
An Argentinian, my heart thrums ablaze,
In awe and wonder, my eyes a fiery glaze,
For Messi, our idol, has led us to glory,
A living god, etched in the nation's story.

The streets now erupt in a sea of celebration,
Flags unfurled, our hearts filled with elation.
For Messi, the blessed soul, we proclaim,
A symbol of unity, honor, and nation's fame.
As tears of joy stream down my face,
I lift my voice, exclaim with grace,
Messi, oh Messi, you've brought us so far,
Our savior, our legend, our guiding star!

In the midst of cheers, Argentina cries,
Overflowing with pride, her spirit flies,
For Messi, her living god, has granted her plea,
In this moment of triumph, her soul is set free.
Oh, Messi, the adored, the nation's delight,
Your presence ignites a fervent light,
In victory, Argentina's hearts align,
For you, our hero, our glory divine.

Determination

In this arduous journey, we find our test,
Hardships and rejections at Destiny's behest.
Each setback, a choice to crumble or persist,
In the face of adversity, shall we desist?

Life's struggles may be ruthless, it is true,
Yet they unveil the strength we never knew.
When beauty and hope seem out of sight,
Resilience and determination must ignite.

Defeat may whisper, urging us to quit,
But deep within, a desire, a fire is lit.
We hold the power to change our course,
To navigate hardships with unwavering force.

The mind, a fortress with dreams in flight,
A realm where dawns are born in the night.
To forge a destiny, we must believe,
In our strength for us to achieve.

When life's burdens weigh upon your chest,
Remember these words and face the test,
For in challenges and hardships, we grow,
With determination, our spirit will forever glow.

Mount Everest

Oh Mount Everest, you mythical demon,
The towering crown so grand,
Endowed with magnetic power,
You beckon climbers to your land.
On your treacherous slopes,
The dangerous thrill they seek,
A quest for name, for glory,
Planting flags atop your icy peak.

But bravely as they ascend
The perilous slopes so high,
They face your demonic power
That often makes them sigh.
Blizzards howl with fury
Of a thousand banshees' cries,
Whipping frostbite's bitter kiss,
Claiming lives beneath the icy skies.

Into the "Death Zone," they venture,
A realm so cold and thin,
Where life hangs by a thread,
Just as the bravest begin.
Hallucinations dance like ghosts,
Tempting the curious mind,
As climbers like Rob Hall
And Fischer, in history we find.

The "Hillary Step" stands proud,
A vertical herculean task,
Where legends like Tenzing
And Hillary dared to unmask.
Their names etched in your lore,
Their triumphs and their tears,
Yet for every victory celebrated,
You reclaim the haunting fears.

We remember Mallory and Irvine,
whose fate remains unknown,
Did they conquer your summit,
What mystery shrouds their bones?
Mount Everest, you wear the earth's crown
Of both allure and despair,
A blend of nature's beauty,
And the risks the brave souls bear.

Oh Mount Everest, you challenge,
You enchant, you claim,
A battleground for human will,
Against nature's untamed game.
May we pay tribute to all those
Who bore the perilous cost,
As you remain an emblem
Of majesty and lives forever lost.

Suffering

In life's crucible, where trials abound,
Suffering and challenges, like flames, surround,
We rise as a majestic phoenix, reborn,
From ashes of struggle, a nobler form.

Each trial endured, a chisel's gentle touch,
Crafting our character, making us clutch
The strength within, the fire in our core,
To face life's tempest, to brave it even more.

Life is a quest for knowledge, a boundless sea,
Each moment a chance to set your spirit free,
Enjoy the journey, don't judge, don't rush,
Reflect and ponder, whenever there's a hush.

For creative souls, these trials are the muse.
They kindle the fire, help us choose
Our language, our expressions, our voice;
In adversity's embrace, we find our choice.

So don't judge the path, its twists and turns,
In every challenge, there's something to learn;
Suffering and trials, they write our song,
For the symphony of life, where we all belong.

Ahmed the Refugee

A land of hardened souls,
Where his cruel fate was cast,
Violence, persecution, poverty,
And haunting ghosts of the past,
Ahmed, a youth with his dreams,
Set forth in a desperate plea,
With few others, sought an escape,
Sailing across the volatile sea.

They embarked on a journey,
Treacherous and bold,
In a small, overcrowded boat,
That was also battered and old.
Barely seaworthy, it sailed away,
Hoping it would somehow fare,
To the shore of salvation,
Beneath the sun's mighty glare.

But in a twist of fate,
A storm's sadistic delight,
Waves began surging high,
plunged them into endless night.
The old boat gave way,
Capsized in the tempest's roar,
Ahmed and his comrades fought,
Struggling for the nearest shore.

Coastguards sailing at a distance
Heard their desperate cries,
Rushed to rescue the drowning souls,
Beneath the dark, fuming skies.
Pulled from the water,
From the sea so wild,
Ahmed and the others,
Every man, woman, and child.

Upon the foreign shore,
Their destination at last,
A place where Ahmed dreamed
His troubles would be past.
But reality proved a shock,
A harsh awakening's sting,
Treated as criminals, since
To this land a burden they'd bring.

Mistrust, scorn, and disdain,
Leave in their hearts a deep scar,
From officials who'd process
Their asylum claims from afar.
A demon's mask on life's face,
Their future shrouded in strife,
Ahmed's dreamland now a nightmare,
He remained stuck in a fragile life.

In the annals of history,
So many Ahmeds remain,
Unsung heroes, in misery,
Who endure unspeakable pain.
Isolation, hunger, atrocities,
It's all their daily fight,
Yet do we truly know them,
Their struggles in the night?

Do we care for their plight,
Do we feel the need for change?
Or do we let these questions,
In our hearts, simply remain strange?
Alas, they linger unanswered,
Like a solemn, distant prayer,
As heroes like Ahmed persevere,
In a world ruthless, malicious, and unfair.

Generations Past

They explored the planet with dreams and fears,
Through triumphs and defeats, joys and tears,
Leaving footsteps in the passage of time,
A legacy of resilience, and strength sublime.
From their homes, they sailed to virgin shores,
Forging ahead, opening so many doors;
With every breath, under dedication's sway,
Each generation thus paved the way.
They worked in fields in hunger's scorn,
Crafting cities, the urban spaces to adorn,
And fought for our rights, for liberty's calls,
Breaking down barriers, tearing down walls.
Generations past transcend the hands of time,
An endless river, a cascading rhyme.

Slavery

In the heart of the city's pulse,
Where dreams should soar,
Buildings stand like sentinels,
But oh, what lies at their core?
Whispers of forgotten souls
Trapped in the stifling air,
Bones, not bricks, compose the frames,
With a scaffold of abysmal despair.

The roads spread like veins,
Carrying the nation's load,
In every step upon their surface
Walks a story left untold.
Rails, they seem to be iron,
Yet old shackles they conceal,
A history of agony and pain,
A truth too painful to heal.

Cities rise like specters grim,
Their foundations built on pain,
A testament to lives consumed,
Like silent tears lost in the rain.
Buildings reach for the heavens' grace,
A yearning to be bold and free,
But if you listen carefully,
You'll hear echoes of a silent plea.

Train tracks weave a tapestry,
A network through the land,
Yet they're orders of oppression,
Guided by an iron hand.
Carriages that transported slaves
Now ferry our dreams along,
Yet, every wheel's revolution
Sings a mournful, haunting song.

Fountains flow with crimson tales,
History's shadows they cast,
Each drop a story of struggles,
Lessons from the distant past.
Blood, not water, fills the basin,
A sacrifice, a torturous scene,
A reminder that our progress stands
On lives of the chained, as it has been.

In the tragic history of humanity,
Our world's facade laid bare,
Unveil bones, not bricks,
A shame now too hard to bear.
But from this shame, let's rise anew,
Acknowledging our ignominious past,
To build a future free from chains,
Where human dignity will forever last.

Children of Earth

From lofty mountains that pierce the sky,
To tranquil valleys where rivers lie,
In Earth's vast and wondrous splendor,
Her divine artistry often made us wonder
At beauty's infinite realm, vividly traced,
We gazed in awe and felt magically embraced.
But Mother Earth, now ravaged by our plunder,
Her stress and agony echo like thunder.
Behold her face and heed her pleas,
Protect her beauty from heinous deeds,
For in a mother's embrace, lies our true worth,
Born from her womb, we are all children of Earth.

Earth's Lament

Climate has turned wretched and wild,
Mother Earth weeps, suffering, defiled.
Her lush landscapes, seared and scorched,
Homes of her children, brutally torched.
Wildfires rage like beasts untamed,
Forest species savagely maimed.
The air heavy with a stifling breath,
Life wilts gasping in the face of death.
Ocean's wrath, a relentless force,
Swallowing homes, dreams, without remorse.
Rivers once flowing, life's sacred streams,
Now run dry like parched, barren gleams.
Their banks so desolate sorrow takes hold,
Arid soils whisper; mournful stories unfold.
Mother Earth's lament, premonitions abound,
To her wretched conditions, her children bound,
Yet, in their greed her anguish they spurn,
Draped in ignorance, no lessons to learn.

Digital Drugs

A laptop with its soft, glowing light,
With a computer genie always in sight,
A modern tale of tethered souls,
In digital realms, their lives unfold.
A mobile in hand, a constant gaze,
Amused and bemused in this digital haze,
Twitter's tweets, Facebook's glow,
A virtual world they've come to know.
Clickbaits lure with flashy charms,
Trading truth for shallow harms,
Likes and shares, the currency of worth,
Yet deeper connections have lost their birth.

Doomscrolling's dance, a tragic play,
Where darkness thrives in endless sway,
A constant stream of woes and fears,
Feeding the minds, infusing tears.
Precious time, once valued gold,
Sinks beneath screens, glittery and bold.
Abundance of distractions, all so rife,
Has woven a tapestry of digital life.
Developed lands with comforts grand,
Grapple with ties that bind like sand.
A paradox of progress is often found,
As minds are lost, connections drowned.

Well, let us pause, look up and see,
The beauty that exists in reality,
For screens may captivate and hold,
Yet life's true wonders are manifold.
In the midst of bytes and endless news,
Let's seek the balance, choose to refuse
The chains that bind us to pixel's bite,
And find the world in natural light.
Since modern times are both a boon and bane,
With shadows that follow our mind's train,
May we navigate this digital sea,
With minds and hearts, once again set free.

Psionic Corps

Psionic corps, a group of souls enlightened,
Gather in silence, their spirit heightened,
Men and women, spiritually advanced,
Bound by a secret, by loyalty entranced.
A government project, shrouded from the light,
To harness their minds, to wield psychic sight,
Thought reading, telepathy, skills they refine,
A journey to realms where spirits intertwine.

They meditate deep, unlocking the mind's door,
Peering into souls, truths they explore.
Yet amidst their progress, fate takes its toll,
A web of deceit, as the story unfolds.
Through powers acquired, they glimpse the truth,
A tangle of lies, the government, a sinister sleuth,
Greed, betrayal, and danger, a treacherous maze,
They confront the leaders, in an ominous haze.

With wisdom and love, their spirits cry out,
A summons to reflect on what life is truly about,
To sever the ignoble ties that bind them to power,
They resign from the game at the decisive hour.
As they step from the shadows, with light in their eyes,
Their spirits unburdened, their conscience their prize,
The leaders stand baffled, their covert plan shaken,
Their power's foundation now shattered and beaten.

Resignation echoes through the corridor's hush,
Leaving the leaders in a quandary, a desperate rush,
For without the psionic weapon, their pursuit is stalled,
In the labyrinth of power, their venal goals forestalled.
In the realms of the paranormal where the corps tread,
'Tis a story of courage, of values, of morals upheld.
Though power and money hold an ever-alluring call,
It is their noble journey, Psionic choose to recall.

My Blue Jeans

Once a symbol of style and flair,
But now stained with tales of despair,
Cheap labor's bitter truth, a haunting refrain,
Oh! My blue jeans have caused such endless pain.
From cotton fields to factories bustling,
Sweatshops where children are struggling,
Child labor's cruel grip, innocence forgotten,
With voices silenced in a maze of cotton.

In Dhaka's slums, where hopes should bind,
Reality's sting, no solace to find,
Families torn apart, for meager pay,
Yet, my blue jeans are here to stay.
Rana Plaza's tragic memory lingers still,
A haunting testament to profiteers' will,
Hundreds trapped, lives crushed in debris,
A cruel reminder of what we fail to see.

Pakistan's looms hum with relentless speed,
Exploited hands weave, on profits we feed,
Low wages, hidden pain in every thread,
As the deprived strive for simple bread.
Rivers tainted blue by dye's toxic dance,
Environmental degradation in a somber trance,
Waste piles high, yet a little regret,
Fast fashion's legacy can we ever forget?

From soil to stitching, a chain of despair,
These stories lead to a solemn prayer,
For change to come, for voices to rise,
To mend the fabric of lives, to empathize.
Can my blue jeans be a call to action,
To seek justice, fairness, and compassion,
In a world where fashion's glow is bright,
Yet doesn't dim the value of human rights?

Hunger

In a world where food should abound,
Yet, a silent storm of hunger swirls around.
Children with sunken eyes and emaciated frames,
Mostly bear the burden of hunger's ruthless games.
Their laughter muted, their spirits worn,
By the gnawing hunger, their lives are burnt.
Mothers, with hollow cheeks and weary sighs,
Search for food beneath unforgiving skies.
Their arms embrace empty promises of care,
Their heavens are covered by clouds of despair.
Fathers, once strong, now weakened, and forlorn,
Struggling to provide, their spirits torn.
In hunger's grip, there's a morality's plea,
Challenges arise, ideologies disagree,
Limited resources impede progress's way,
The powerful turn blind, darkness holds sway.

Stop the Cycles

Parents scream, fierce tempers ignite.
Children's innocence consumed by fright.
Bodies bruised, souls battered, torn,
Love's absence replaced by anger's scorn.
Cries muffled behind closed doors,
Little hearts robbed, dreams no more.
Invisible scars, etched deep within.
A childhood deprived, a haunting sin.
Alas!
Tempered by anger, their fates are sealed.
Scars unseen, their wounds never healed.
Oblivious to cycles these parents perpetuate,
Creating violent adults, a society's weight,
Social deformities formed, dark seeds sown,
The cycles of abuse callously grown.
For hardened souls, the pain is passed down.
It's a legacy of torment, groans, wrath, and frown.

Police Brutality

In a somber, disturbing scene, we behold
Police brutality's tale, dark and cold.
Flashing lights, blue and red, flare
Lingering tension, heavy in the air.
Night illuminated, eerie glow,
Upon the darkness, a chilling show.
With anger's voices, agony's cries,
Injustice and pain echoed in the skies,
Ensues in street mayhem of despair,
Trust shattered, fragments everywhere.
Aaaaaaaaaaaaaa!!!
A crowd assembles, faces masked,
Disbelief and fear tightly clasped,
Witnessing power's cruel abuse,
Sinister cops, their minds obtuse.
Victim's pleas for mercy unheard,
A body lies like a wounded bird.
Systemic woes, deep-rooted pain,
Through streets, they reverberate disdain.
Yet, in this sorrow, a fervent plea,
For change, justice, and equality.

Son of a Bitch

Amidst the bustling streets,
I just walk a world apart,
A homeless soul with weary feet,
I carry a wounded heart.
Public transport's cold reception,
Its seats a distant dream,
I stand among the shadows,
A ghost in this grand scheme.

A sour scent lingers with me,
Like the weight of my own past,
An odor born from circumstances,
A brutal burden meant to last.
Hushed whispers in public spaces,
As I'm met with wary eyes,
They all look away, and crinkle noses,
As if there's no truth behind my cries.

"Homeless" they murmur softly,
"Scumbag," "bastard" upon their lips,
"Bum," "tramp," "rough sleeper" etc.,
The names are just a cruel eclipse.
But no monikers can capture
All that lies within my soul,
Behind this worn and ragged facade,
A tragic tale in broken folds.

Police officers in uniforms,
Protectors of the peace,
Yet, some forget compassion,
As their cruelty doesn't cease.
"Son of a bitch!" they curse at me,
For I'm less than a whole,
Reducing me to profanities
That brutally cut into my soul.

But still, I rise above the scorn,
A spirit strong and true,
My identity transcends the names,
The biases they all spew.
For every insult hurled my way,
I hold onto my dignity, my grace,
A reminder of my hidden worth,
Despite life's ruthless, unfair pace.

So, call me what you like, dear world,
My self-respect will be held high,
A human being with a real story,
Beneath the open, wonderful sky.
With grit in my soul, I'll survive
Despite the world's cruel itch,
For deep within this homeless heart,
Beats more than just a "son of a bitch."

To Be Kind or to Be Right

> The quality of mercy is not strain'd.
> It droppeth as the gentle rain from heaven
> Upon the place beneath. It is twice blest:
> It blesseth him that gives and him that takes.
> —WILLIAM SHAKESPEARE, The Merchant of Venice

In the matter of choices,
A path we must tread,
Between being kind or being right,
Where our thoughts are led.
Wisdom dictates a principle,
A truth simple and profound—
Choose kindness always,
And right you will be found.

Since pursuing being right,
We may lose our way,
Lured by ego's sway,
The dreadful price we pay.
But kindness, a beacon
That guides our sight,
Unveils the path where
Truth and love unite.

Since kindness sows
Understanding's seed,
It softens hearts, bridges gaps,
And mends the creed.
'Tis through kindness,
Bonds of harmony grow,
And righteousness, with empathy,
Does naturally flow.

Rape

In the depths of man, a monstrous tide,
Lurks some darkness that cannot hide
A tendency vile, repugnant, and cruel,
A savage instinct and a wicked fuel.
It is not in nature but in a twisted mind,
That such abhorrence it seeks to find,
A perversion born of power and control,
A gruesome urge that takes its toll.
Inflamed by anger, and bestial desire,
It tramples on souls, leaving hearts afire.
With innocence shattered, and trust betrayed,
Sacred Womanhood weeps forever dismayed.

Love is Not for Sale

In morning's light, a man is seen,
Dressed in a bathrobe, looks very keen,
At a bordello's bureau, with a cigar in hand,
Perusing a newspaper, a la-la land.

An advert pops up, catches him cold.
A book's cover, its title bold,
"Love is not for sale," it does claim.
His heart trembles, his soul aflame.

He stubs his cigar, his face aglow,
His thoughts in turmoil, emotions flow.
His eyes are glued to the advert's core.
What does life, for him, have in store?

Love can no longer be bought,
A future unknown, his mind fraught.
He ponders options he'll explore,
When love is elusive forevermore.

A Zookeeper's Song

In nature's sprawl, wherever lights fall,
There dwell creatures, both grand and small,
Our little brothers and sisters so dear,
Yet we deny them a place within our sphere.

Oh, how oblivious we are to their grace,
Deaf to their cries, their pleas in this space!
Within our hearts, remorse doesn't bloom,
As brutes we are, inflicting cruelty's doom.

Oh, where's our aesthetics, our souls' decree,
To cherish the beauty in every animal we see?
Where are our ethics, our feelings' beat,
Why this cruelty's triumph, humanity's defeat?

Lord, send forth Thy chosen son once more,
To redeem mankind from its decadent core.
In a world driven by selfish desire's worth,
Restore harmony for all creatures on earth.

Mumba

In twilight's golden shade, Mumba the Cheetah played,
Prowling and dancing to the savanna's serenade.
With a gazelle in her jaws, her pride shining bright,
Mumba returned to her cubs in the day's fading light.

But as she drew near, a dreadful sight she'd see,
Her little cubs, so dear, lost to brutality.
The lions had struck, with heartless might,
Leaving pain and despair in that desolate night.

Tears mingled with blood, sorrow in her eyes,
She licked those cold bodies, love's last goodbye.
Her kill forgotten, her dinner untouched,
In acute grief, her heartstrings were clutched.

Amidst the shadows, she wept for her kin,
In the silence, her tragedy, a tale of loss within.
Her lament filled the air, a cry of grief,
As she mourned in despair, her heart sought relief.

Her world shattered by fate, in anguish, Mumba cried,
The stars bore witness to a mother's love denied.
Through the darkest of night, Mumba mourned,
Her lament tailed off, as a new dawn broke adorned.

Hank and His Rocky

In the Wild West where the prairies sprawl,
It's a story of a cowboy, proud and tall,
Hank, confident of his youth, his manly stride,
With his horse named Rocky, always by his side.
Hank and Rocky—they made quite a pair,
Riding through the prairies without a care,
They galloped through the land wild and free,
A magnificent sight for everyone to see.

With every hoofbeat, their spirit soared,
As they traversed lands, Hank never bored,
A cowboy, so relaxed, cool, and conceited too,
With passion and joy in every ride he knew.
But Fate, as fickle as the wind's swift gust,
Wrote a different tale, filled with mistrust,
As Rocky fell ill and his strength did wane,
Proud Hank had to face an unbearable pain.

The final fateful day, against the somber skies,
Hank stood by Rocky, with tears in his eyes.
In the quiet of twilight, with a heart full of dread,
He raised his pistol high, to Rocky's noble head.
The shot rang out, a thunderclap in the night,
And Rocky fell silent, no more in the fight.
With the loss of Rocky, his soul torn apart,
As Hank felt it, his heart pierced by a dart.

As he climbed into bed, his emotions did collide,
Images of Rocky swirled majestic and wild.
Hank buried his face, his pillow soaked in tears,
A knight, a gallant cowboy, now filled with fears,
For Rocky was more than a horse, he could see,
A friend, a companion, a part of his identity.
In the heart of the cowboy, in the depths of his soul,
It was a tale of his love that would never grow old.

Jane and Aunt Becky

In a quiet, small town, 'twas a story old,
Young Jane, a student with a heart of gold.
She cared for Becky, an elderly woman truly meek,
And it was Jane's company, Becky would always seek.
Through days and nights, they shared their tales,
Jane's youthful dreams, Becky's life's travails.
A bond so strong, like kin they had grown,
Old Becky, in her heart, called Jane her own.

"Dear Aunt Becky," Jane would sweetly say,
As she cared for her, day by day.
She nursed her through twilight's gentle grace,
Their connection, a bond no time could erase.
But Jane's dreams and ambitions began to soar,
As her studies led her to distant shores.
Five years flew by like a fleeting song,
Until she returned, where she had once belonged.

Once again, she sought Aunt Becky's embrace,
But dementia's diabolic hand had taken its place.
With each passing day, memories slipped away,
Aunt Becky, once vibrant, now in a shadowy gray.
Jane held photos, moments frozen in time,
Trying to rekindle that spark so sublime.
But the light in Becky's eyes had grown dim,
The past faded away like a distant hymn.

Tears welled up in Jane's grieving eyes,
As she realized the truth, a painful surprise.
Senility's cruel hand had stolen the key,
To unlock the treasure of their shared memory.
She left Aunt Becky, her heart heavy as stone,
Reflecting on life's cycles, as is often known.
Impermanence, mortality, they whispered in the air,
Reminding her of the love they both used to share.

Oh Tragedy!

Oh Tragedy, devoid of empathy's grace,
Unfeeling specter, no tears on your face.
You stole my joy, my love, my very breath,
With callous ease, you sentenced me to death.
No tears now flow, for my eyes are dry,
My emotions numbed, I couldn't even cry.
Laughter fades, as life seems hollow and frail.
Mocking echoes, while you, Tragedy, cruelly prevail.

September 11th, My Final Moments

On September 11th morning,
High above the bustling ground,
I was sitting on the 80th floor,
Quiet, contemplative, not a sound.
The proud, dignified World Trade Center,
A symbol of corporate might,
Little did I know it was awaiting
A fateful, calamitous plight.

Out of the blue, a thunderous jolt,
A massive explosion loud and clear,
Smoke and dust filling the room,
It was chaotic, dire, dark, and severe.
My voice strangled, my throat choking,
Towards the nearest window, I raced,
Only to be filled with horror and witness
The tower, in a smoky cloud, encased.

Across the floor a ball of fire,
Like an unrelenting, raging beast,
Devoured everything in its path,
Burning wrath that never ceased.
Trapped in this nightmare,
While the walls closing in,
I felt the end drawing near,
A new journey I had to begin.

With my courage faltering,
And my hopes brutally crushed,
I made that dreadful decision,
My voice forever to be hushed—
Jumping out the window,
The only avenue I could see,
To escape the fiery inferno,
To finally set myself free.

Teeth clenched, Goodbye, I spluttered,
To all I loved, quietly in my mind,
As I prepared to take the leap,
Leaving the whole world behind.
With despair, resignation, and horror,
A vacuous mind, a crying heart entwined,
In that fateful, pivotal moment,
Death seemed sacred, majestic, eternally enshrined.

Through smoke, dust, and fire,
I took the decisive, fatal flight,
As Mother Earth embraced me,
I succumbed to Destiny's might.
Alas, so many souls were lost,
In this tragedy's atrocious art!
A day etched in a nation's memory,
Of its history, being eternally a part.

BOOK II

Romantic Verses

Birth of Venus

In Botticelli's timeless art, a marvel is born,
A divine birth for five hundred years adorned.
Enchanting us, as if it's still Botticelli's prime,
A masterpiece rising beyond our earthly time.

Frozen in time, a divinity graced by light,
Venus emerges from the foamy sea's delight,
With innocence draped in gentle folds,
And virginity preserved in hues of gold.

Elegance drips from each cascading curl,
A zephyr's whispers, a mesmerizing whirl,
Sublime femininity in every curve and line,
The form of a muse so exquisitely defined!

Veiled in sensuality, like morning's soft kiss,
Yet in her gaze, it's a touch of eternal bliss.
Each brush stroke, a dance so divine,
Capturing allure in an immortal design.

Venus transcends—the canvas and the frame,
Through centuries, a virgin beauty reigns the same,
For in Birth of Venus, she lives eternally anew,
A symbol of love, seduction, and beauty, forever true.

On the Walls of My Heart

On the walls of my heart, your name is etched,
Inscribed in love's ink, forever sketched.
A portrait of you on my soul's canvas gleams,
In vibrant hues, it's more than just dreams.
In solitude, your voice with its gentle might,
A comforting refrain, in the quiet of the night,
Whispering secrets, like a cherished song,
It lingers in the stillness where you belong.

Oh beloved, your name on every wall of my heart,
A love so profound, my devotion, my work of art!

In quiet moments, I breathe your scent so sweet,
A fragrant memory, my heart skips a beat.
I feel your presence, though we're far apart,
In the depths of my soul, you're my muse, my art.
A flame of passion, it burns deep and true,
In every part of you, in all that you do,
Your neck, your graceful curve, an ardent embrace,
Your hand, your fingers, love's tender trace.

Oh beloved, your name on every wall of my heart,
A love so profound, my devotion, my work of art!

With all my heart's strength, this love I proclaim,
In every nuance, it's more than a life's frivolous game.
It's the melody of our souls, forever intertwined,
In the tapestry of love, in every thread that I find.
Oh beloved, in you, my heart has found its home,
In every corner of my being, you eternally roam.
I feel you with my love, fierce, unbound, and true,
With every fiber of my being, I belong to you.

Oh beloved, your name on every wall of my heart,
A love so profound, my devotion, my work of art!

Sunset on the Vltava

Beneath the setting sun's warm, golden charm
Sitting by the Vltava, as I touch your tender arm,
Floating in streams of time, memories unfurl,
Of a distant evening, love's enchanting swirl.

The Vltava, a silent witness to love's softest rhyme,
Holding secrets of whispered promises, through time.
Its mirrored surface, a canvas serene and divine,
Reflects our love's hues, in the sun's warm shine.

Buskers' melodies, a symphony of the heart,
In urban bedlam, where love found its start.
Amidst the cacophony, our souls were in flight,
Hearts beating in harmony under a fading light.

Traffic's distant roar, once a dissonant sound,
Now a part of the memory, forever profound,
For love persists through chaos and peace,
A bond that grows, its wonders never cease.

Ducks and swans, with graceful rhythms, glide,
In their peaceful journey, side by side.
A symbol of love's timeless grace,
In life's streams, they too have a place.

Oh beloved, this moment, a testament so true,
To love's enduring power, between me and you,
Earthly and yet ethereal, forever it shall be,
A dream and a memory, for eternity.

Scarlet Cloud

Oh beloved, the scarlet cloud of the sunset,
Painted with the blood of my desire,
You float freely in the heavens of my soul,
A celestial dance, my passion's fire.

Your scarlet lips, a portal to my sensuous flame,
In shades of vibrant purple, they paint my dreams,
A melody of love, melded with the sunset,
Flow through my heart in my passion's streams.

The scarlet cloud kisses the golden sun.
Her radiant love burns bright in the sky.
She colors my heart, my amorous play,
And inflames my breath like a lover's sigh.

Oh beloved, in your allure, I find my muse,
Each word I write is a tribute to love so true,
You are the scarlet cloud of my heart,
A love so deep that it paints my world anew.

Shrouded Moon

In the velvet heavens, shrouded Moon weeps,
Cloaked in shadows, tragic secrets she keeps.
Her light, a fading glow in the ebony night,
Like a dim lamp in a Persian tale's delight.

With a phantom's smile behind a gossamer veil,
And a lover's whisper on the midnight trail,
Shrouded Moon is a mistress of disguise,
Yet within her heart, some tragedy lies.

Oh shrouded Moon, in your enigmatic grace,
You cast a spell on this endless space,
A realm of dreams, both near and far,
You guide us through the night, to a distant star.

Let the cloud's veil softly caress your face,
Embrace the mystique, the endless chase,
For in your shrouded glow, I find my tune,
A dance, a trance, oh my beloved shrouded Moon.

Starry Night

The ink-soaked vault of nocturnal glow,
Stars, like silver bees, in a mystical show,
No veil of clouds, their beauty so grand,
Under a spangled shawl, bewitched I stand.
Each star, a lantern in eternity's hall,
A menacing universe, a dreamy pall.
As the welkin reveals the Creation's face,
I'm lost in time, in a boundless space.
On an ocean of stars, I sail without a shore,
Drifting on the starlit waves forevermore.
Mystic whispers, life's ancient lore unfurl,
I dance among the galaxies, a divine whirl.
No earthly ties for my spirit's flight,
As I dissolve into the endless night,
A speck, yet part of the universe so grand,
What a spectacle on the shore of this cosmic land!

Astral City

In a world beyond the mundane,
The astral city gleams bright,
A tapestry of dreams aglow,
As day dissolves into night.
Its towers reach celestial heights,
Adorned with stardust rare,
As if the cosmos weaved its lights
Into each spire and every flare.

Within its moonlit streets,
Lights and shadows softly play,
Like whispers of forgotten times
That would dance the night away.
Ethereal lights in every hue
Like fireflies in their flight,
They paint the skies with vibrant blue,
And pierce the velvet veil of the night.

The air is crisp and redolent
With the scent of exotic blooms.
They're seductive in their fragrance,
With secrets in their silken plumes.
Enchanted gardens filled with allure,
Where celestial crystals gently chime,
The petals woven through time and space,
Eternity in this Elysian clime.

Into this magical, mystical realm,
Where I'm borne in a dreamy flight,
A city on the astral plane where
Angels and cherubs joyously unite.
I wander through the streets,
And lie in soft moonbeams;
As life and magic gently meet,
I'm lost in a world of dreams.

Oh Cloud

In the cerulean stretch of endless skies,
Oh Cloud, the happiest soul, you rise,
Unburdened, you drift in a carefree flight,
Aimlessly wandering in sheer delight.

You wander above the world's disdain,
Escaping the tumult, the struggle, the pain.
From lofty realms, you gaze below,
Only to view a world, a radiant glow.

Oh Cloud, the guardian of the poets, aloft,
In your touch, the bitter is sweetened oft.
You never could see the world's cruel strife,
As you float in the hues of harmonious life.

While we choke in the grip of greed,
A dark dance of corruption and need,
You waltz through the heavens, untouched, serene,
In your ethereal world, grand, pristine.

The viciousness of man's nature concealed,
A sight where nothing but beauty is revealed.
No squalor, no ugliness taints your views,
Only a riveting kaleidoscope of marbled hues.

Oh Cloud, the happiest soul, you soar,
Above the chaos, the drama, forevermore,
May we borrow your feathery wings and rise,
To drink in the beauty from the skies.

Ich Liebe dich, I Love You

(Inspired by Beethoven's "Ich Liebe Dich, So Wie Du Mich")

In joys and sorrows, you've stood by my side,
A true companion in life's tumultuous ride.
In times of anguish, to you I cling,
To my aching heart, a solace you bring.

In morning's light, with your presence near,
Love's essence swirls in a mist of cheer.
As evening descends and you grace the scene,
Love's fragrance lingers like perfume serene.

The spring breeze whispers with love unfurled,
Caressing my soul like the sweetest of worlds.
With tears of joy, I walk in the rain,
And fill my heart with a joyous refrain.

Humbly I beseech the angels above,
Shower blessings upon you, pure and true love.
Guard you from evils with all their might,
And keep our souls forever gently alight.

Petrin Hill

On Petrin's slope where time stands still,
I walk in raptures—a romantic thrill.
Each step, a journey through days long gone,
The stories of my love, the golden dawn.

Winding paths and cobblestone lanes,
Echoes of laughter, love's sweet refrains.
Leaves ooze secrets, trees gently sway,
Recalling our innocence, bright days of May.

Birds in the sky, with their dulcet choir,
To harmonious notes, our souls would aspire.
As melodies filled the tranquil space,
A love story was written in every trace.

Atop the hill's brow, we stood hand in hand,
A view of Prague, like a dreamscape grand,
Rooftops and medieval spires, oh, what a sight!
Our love reflected in Prague's golden twilight.

The garden of time, where memories bloom,
A place where love escapes its earthly tomb,
The mystique of the hill, like tales of old,
Love of two souls, a story eternally retold.

Autumn Melancholy

Amidst autumn's hues, a bittersweet refrain,
A labyrinth of memories, love's subtle pain.
Golden leaves fall like whispers of the past,
Each one a moment, too beautiful to last.

In every rustling breeze, I hear her name,
A haunting echo, my passion, my old flame.
The warmth we shared, now a distant ember,
Yet her memories paint my heart's September.

Beneath the canopies, scarlet and gold,
A touch of secrets, sacred and old.
In every shade, mystique so serene,
Streams of emotions, oh, my desire's queen!

The maple trees reflect the love I knew,
Once ablaze with passion, a vibrant hue.
Soon branches will be bare, like my arms tonight,
I long to hold her again, oh! in my senses' might.

The season has changed, yet my heart's the same,
Missing her deeply, my passion, my old flame.
That loving face, the eyes, the enchanting gleam,
On memory's canvas, forever they would beam.

Adieu

Amidst tearful nights, love finds its way,
A journey of a soul, I would seek a brighter day.
In solitude's comfort, I'd learn to mend,
For it takes lonely tears for me to transcend.

In the forest of passion, my spirit will roam,
Seeking the path back to where love calls home.
Accepting the inevitable, the end drawing near,
I'll accept the truth with humility, my dear.

In my heart, I've imprisoned love in too many cages.
Yet the pain is too deep, like a tempest that rages.
Life is still a mystery, as struggles unfold.
For now, acceptance of defeat must take hold.

With the strength to move forward, I bid adieu,
Choosing growth and healing, starting anew.
Though we go separate ways, love's story remains,
As I release the pain and break these chains.

My First Love

In the garden of your heart, I often roam,
Amidst the blooms of memories, seeking a home.
Oh my first love, a gentle echo of the past,
I wonder if those moments can forever last.
Do they still linger by that river's edge,
Or are they lost like words on a forgotten page?
Perhaps they're like footprints in the sand,
Washed away by the tides, erased by the land.
Yet I have hope, like a rainbow in the sky,
Traces of our love still in your heart lie;
The sweet moments we shared, like stars in the night,
In the web of your dreams, still burn bright.
Though time may flow like an endless stream,
In the depths of my heart, love remains a dream.
And if you ever wonder, if you ever do,
Know that in my heart, I still care for you.

Aline

(Inspired by Christophe's "Aline")

On sandy shores, her sweet face I drew,
A smile that warmed my heart, a love so true!
But as it rained, and all was washed away,
Her presence vanished, lost to my heart's dismay.

On my memory's canvas too I painted her face,
but Life's storms came, and they did erase
That smiling charm I held so dear.
Again, she left me, in doubt and fear.

In the garden where I once made her cry,
Flowers still bloom and birds still fly,
But without her touch, there's no cheer,
No smiles in blossoms, no songs I hear.

Upon this path, her spirit once dwelled,
Now she's gone, nowhere to be held.
Everywhere I searched, but she eluded my sight,
Lost like a shipwreck, Oh! my soul's plight!

Aline, my dear, I cry, please come back to me.
My heart weeps for your love, why can't you see?
There's a deep emptiness that only you can mend.
In your arms, this heartache will find its end.

Lament of Orpheus

In the bleak netherworld where spirits weep,
Orpheus, with his lyre, takes an odyssey deep,
To the throne of Hades, he makes his way,
His grieving heart trembling in a tragic sway.
With each mournful note, his music fills the air,
A lament for Eurydice, ensnared in Hades's lair.
His voice, filled with anguish, flows with tears,
As he sings of his love through endless years.
"O Hades, lord of this somber domain,
Let my love be free from thy chain.
Eurydice, my soul's eternal flame,
Without her, I am only an inferno's name."
Words resonate with poetry, a heartfelt plea,
To release his beloved, to set her spirit free.
In the eyes of Hades and Queen Persephone,
A glimmer of compassion, a glint of sympathy,
Yet unyielding fate, its course already set,
Eurydice becomes a vision Orpheus can't forget.
His lament, a haunting melody so divine,
A beacon of devotion that'll always shine.
In his mournful song, in his soulful cry,
His love lives on, beyond Death's frigid sigh.

Tantric Union

Two hearts, in a temple of union, intertwine,
In tantric realms, both earthly and divine,
Holistic flames ignite in a fervent quest,
For body, mind, and soul to find a nest.
It's not just flesh, but souls clung tight,
A fusion of elements, in passion's might.
With a gentle touch, emotions cascade,
A mélange of senses that doesn't fade.
From the deepest core to the spirits above,
The eternal mysteries of celestial love
Transcend the physical, as we journey far,
To share our breath with planets and stars.
Tantric union is a bridge to the divine,
Two souls as one, in bliss, they shine.

Your Eyes

In a world veiled by the mystic night,
It's a passion's delight that you ignite.
Locked in this moment, our souls entwined,
Your eyes are captive to my hunger blind.
In the glint of your eyes, I see a star gleam;
Lost I become, lost within a dream.
No words can capture what my heart would say,
So let my eyes be the ones to convey,
In their silent words, let Love be an art,
In a bond divine, we shall never part.

Vicissitudes

On the storm's path, my trails were laid,
Through joys and sorrows, life's journey swayed.
On the flood's path too, I often remained,
Afloat in life's tide, laughter and tears unchained.

In life's landscape, my love appeared, unforeseen,
Like floodwaters rushing, a spirit blithe and keen.
In the blazing sun, we cherished days so bright,
Yet with the darkest clouds, we faced the gloomy night.

I built castles of dreams, swept away by storms,
Enchanting visions shattered—by reality's norms.
Now I reminisce about this life's journey so vast,
With trails left behind in the echoes of the past.

As memories of spring, in autumn leaves, abide,
I carry in my heart this life's tales far and wide.
Strength in the tempest and solace in the breeze,
I've learned to embrace the tides with remorseless ease.

Non, Je Ne Regrette Rien, No Regret

(Inspired by Edith Piaf's "Non, Je Ne Regrette Rien")

On the shore of time, as I bravely stand,
No regret for how Destiny held my hand.
Blissful and tragic moments, they intertwine,
They are all the same, in this heart of mine.

Love, once a prince, adorned the day's throne,
But on another, a pauper, as it was known.
Sweetest honey it bestowed with delight,
Yet bitterest bile, it revealed in its spite.

But I hold no grudge for the days gone by,
I cast away memories, bid them goodbye.
Pleasures and troubles, now all erased,
My heart's a clean slate, its worries effaced.

My past is now buried, along with its pain,
In the ashes of time, it shall forever remain.
For a fresh start, this dawn I claim,
In the morning sun, I find a new golden flame.

La Vie en Rose, Through Rose-Colored Glasses

(Inspired by Edith Piaf's "La Vie en Rose")

Life, through rose-colored glasses, I perceive,
As your lips meet mine, and your eyes me deceive.
Heaven's sighs, angels' breath, I feel upon my face,
When your kiss transports me to that sacred space.
Drawn to your heart, in the rose garden I stroll,
Where butterflies dance, embracing my soul.
Your voice, a melody from the cerulean skies,
An angel's song, with every word that flies,
Give me your heart, your soul, heed my plea,
Through rose-colored glasses, life as I see.

Solitude

It's a tranquil time with poetic grace,
The air of silence fills my space,
A haven where whispers softly weave
A rich world within, a profound reprieve.

When stillness with the quietude meets,
Time slows down, and worries retreat,
The cluttered chaos of the bustling crowd,
Replaced by tranquility, a mystic shroud.

In a realm of introspection, thoughts ascend,
Exalted feelings and moods transcend.
No masks to wear, no pretense to maintain,
Authenticity flows, free from disdain.

The music of solitude with its haunting refrain
Is a melody that nourishes the spirit's domain.
In stillness, we find the essence of our core,
And discover the love for ourselves forevermore.

Adagio, Slowly

(Inspired by Tomaso Albinoni's "Adagio")

I seek but can't find you near,
A whisper in the wind, your voice I hear.
A soul with a heart shattered and blue,
Awaits the day, my love, when I meet you, Adagio!

The nights without your tender touch,
Dreams without stars, I miss you so much!
Visions of your face, hopes anew,
Destiny will lead my soul to you, Adagio!

Within me unfolds a melody I've composed,
For you, my love, where you're enclosed.
If you know where, if you know how
I am, my love, embrace me now, Adagio!

The sun seems pale without your gleam,
Write your name in the sky, in love's theme.
Tell me, I'm your everything, your muse,
In you I'll find a new life to choose, Adagio!

Lost I am without your touch,
Reveal your heart, let me clutch,
Let me believe, you are my melody,
Let the music set me forever free, Adagio!

My Twin Flame

In her eyes, I glimpse a timeless universe,
A mirror of a past life, an Elysian traverse,
Her gaze, like a constellation, familiar and sublime,
As if our souls once danced in an ancient, distant time.

Her scent, a fragrant echo, elusive and sweet,
A memory of a garden where we'd meet,
Inhaling whispers of a love I can't explain,
As if our souls converged on a long-forgotten plane.

Her voice, a melody from dreams of yesteryears,
A symphony of echoes that silence all my fears,
Each word, as if a verse we've always known,
In a world where our spirits eternally have grown.

In dreams, she lingers, in realms of slumber's grace,
A glimpse of a past life, an enigmatic trace,
Our hearts, bound by a force no eyes can see,
A love that transcends death, for all eternity.

This intense attraction defies Time's cruel hand,
The harrowing trials of life, it humbly withstands.
Beyond the grave, I'd cherish her, my eternal flame,
And in every life, she's the one I'll always claim.

A Poet's Gift

My poetry, a balm to heal your sorrow's sting,
Is the melody to lift your heart and make it sing.
It'll adorn your neck like a necklace fine.
It'll wrap you like a silk shawl sweet divine.
It will gently swirl around your heart,
To render your life, on a sunny day, an art,
And flow through your soul like silent tears,
When you are out in a field and rain appears.
The fragrance will waft through verses, pleasing you true,
Look in my eyes, my love, as you read these words anew.
When distance separates us, and I am far away,
My words will embrace you, every moment, every day.
And as I depart from this world and my voice is stilled,
My poetry, in your heart, will slowly build
An echo of my loving voice resonating still,
A timeless connection, bound by love's gentle will.

BOOK III

War

Ukraine War, a Reflection

A tempest gathers, venomous flames ignite,
Forgotten virtues, and hubris at its height.
With bonds of kinship torn asunder,
Humanity's demise echoes like thunder.
The skies are weeping, mourning our plight,
Witnessing the horror, the endless night.
Nature shudders, her wounds so deep,
Tears of anguish, you can hear her weep.
In pride and greed, blind ambition's sway,
With humanity's face in a tragic display,
As the Apocalypse beckons a somber refrain,
We all seem to be bound in tragedy's chain.

Blood

In veins of life, streams run,
A scarlet thread, where the journey's begun,
Like branches reaching far and wide,
It nourishes, sustains deep inside.
Through arteries like canals it flows,
A lifeline where its essence grows,
To every corner, every cell,
Vibrations where secrets dwell.

But oh, blood on our hands, a stain we wear,
A mark of shame, a burden we bear.

The heart, a forge of fiery beat,
Where blood's red river finds its seat,
Pumping life with rhythmic grace,
A vital force, a sacred space.
But our hearts are more than flesh,
Every throb, a compassion's mesh.
Blood that courses through our veins
Should carry love, not bitter stains.

But oh, blood on our hands, a stain we wear,
A mark of shame, a burden we bear.

Let us have hearts that are pure,
With empathy and love that can cure
Our ailments in every body part,
Let kindness flow to all cells from the heart.
Embrace the pulse, the steady flow,
Of life's red river as it goes,
Through every fiber, every hue,
A gift of grace for me and you.

But oh, blood on our hands, a stain we wear,
A mark of shame, a burden we bear.

In body and spirit, let love prevail,
A healing touch that cannot fail.
As we connect heart to heart,
Let understanding be our souls' art.
Let us weave a tapestry
Of blood and love in unity,
For a symphony of life's grand plan,
Where blood is divine and pure in man.

But oh, blood on our hands, a stain we wear,
A mark of shame, a burden we bear.

War

Oh War, you a monster of sorrow,
    A chapter in humanity's darkest tale.
A false promise you let the future borrow,
    Leaving devastation in your fearsome trail.

Cloaked in the spurious notion of glory,
    As if bloodshed could ever bring us peace.
With your twisted narrative, a sad story,
    Where love and compassion find no release.

Oh War, you a thief of innocent dreams,
    You claim the lives of the brave and the weak,
Leaving tears that flow in bloody streams,
    And scars on hearts that forever speak.

Cursed and scorned, nations crumble, divide,
    Families are torn apart, shattered by strife.
Your devouring flames leave no one to hide,
    With haunting memories lasting for life.

May your ruinous reign soon come to an end.
    May nations rise above your treacherous call.
May compassion and understanding ascend.
    May sanity and peace prevail for one and all.

A Soldier's Adieu

In the twilight's somber shade, they stand,
A soldier resolute, and his wife, hand in hand.
The weight of uncertainty bears heavy and deep,
As they face the night where Fate's secrets creep.

His uniform is adorned with pride and strife,
His heart torn between duty and his cherished wife.
In the eyes that meet, there's passion tender and bold;
But deep in their hearts, grim stories of war unfold.

Amidst the shadows, their whispered vows,
With promises etched on furrowed brows,
He gently touches her tear-stained cheek,
His love for her, words could barely speak.

"The distant lands beckon me to come,
Oh my love, do you hear the war drum?
In your arms, even a gray day looks so bright,
A sanctuary of love, with endless light!"

In her heart, there is a drumming sound,
An echo of love's rhythm, that binds 'em round.
Yet in her eyes, a strength so fierce,
A warrior's true wife, devoid of fears.

Letter from the Front Line

Dear leaders, hear my fervent plea,
From depths of suffering, I write to thee.
In this world of pain, where hope is thin,
Withdraw from war, let compassion win.
I've witnessed horrors that none should see,
The cost of conflict, the price of enmity.
Beneath the gray skies of despair,
I beg for mercy, a world to repair.
Each drop of blood, each anguished cry,
Resounds like a plea, reaching the sky,
Livelihood lost, dreams turned to dust,
In humanity, please place your trust.
The nights are cold, the days are long,
As I write these words, my spirit's strong,
But time is short, the hour is near,
To end this suffering, to quell the fear.
In this earnest plea, I lay my soul,
A captive heart yearning for the goal,
To see an end to this grim crusade,
And pave a path where peace is laid.
Oh leaders, let wisdom reign,
And spare us all this endless bane,
For in the end, what shall we gain,
But ruins vast and lingering pain?
Oh leaders, let compassion guide,

Put arrogance, vanity, and pride aside,
No more to suffer, no more to mourn,
In ending the war, let humanity be reborn.

The Scar

In the gnarled hand of this war-worn soul,
Lies a tale of battle that took its toll.
A scar, etched deep, tells a story profound,
Of friendship forged on sacred ground.
In the heat of conflict, under skies dark gray,
We two stood, side by side, that fateful day,
A brotherhood born in the crucible of strife,
Where courage, not medals, defined our life.
I reached out to save, in that moment of dread,
As shrapnel rained down and the sky bled red.
The price I'd pay is etched in flesh and bone,
But in that act of valor, a bond was sown.
Our hearts now beat as one in battles we brave,
A bond unbreakable, in the face of the grave.
The scar, a testament, not merely skin-deep,
But etched in the tales of promises we keep.
The scar, a symbol of the love that abides,
In a warrior's heart, where courage strides.

Sophie's Choice

Her eyes, pools of sorrow, tell the tale—
With a burden so heavy, no soul can prevail,
In Auschwitz's darkness, where demons reign,
She faces a choice, soaked in horror's rain.

It's a tale of mother's love, fierce and true,
Two precious souls, her heart once knew,
Her anguished plea, a tear-stained voice,
To save one child, while condemning the choice.

With trembling hands, she embraces her plight,
Selecting one, on that woeful, chilling night.
Her little girl, her life, left to an unknown fate,
A mournful choice, a pain that wouldn't abate.

Haunted by echoes of that tragic day,
She carries the weight under remorse's sway.
The scars she bears, etched deep within,
A cruel reminder of an unwitting, hapless sin.

Warship to Worship

A letter's small shift, and wisdom as our guide,
Humanity's clarion call, and a universe we decide,
In a sanctum of unity, where revenge is undone,
And the glow of fraternity is the new rising sun.

No battles for dominance, no cries of despair,
Just a refrain of compassion rises in the air.
Paradise on this earth, to bloom and to thrive,
As peace, harmony, and love are well alive.

Gone are the cannons, their thunderous roar,
Replaced by the hymns that we all can adore.
In its worship, humanity shall unite,
Illumed by beams from wisdom's light.

We roam the landscapes, blessed with divine grace,
Humanity bows, as the pilgrims humbly fill the space.
Raise our awareness, Lord, give enlightenment a birth,
Bring Paradise to earth through your infinite worth.

With your love our light, and compassion our art,
We'll mend the rifts that are tearing us apart.
From warship to worship, your grace we implore,
Bring Paradise to earth, forever and more.

Om Shanti, Oh Peace!

In this garden of life where souls are born,
Let there be peace and love, the sacred corn,
Let happiness bloom like flowers in the spring,
And joy be the song all hearts will sing.

Let the river of compassion, its meandering course,
Through the heart of Earth, flow with unbridled force,
Carve a path of empathy, eroding hatred's shore,
Binding every heart in unity, Lord, we implore.

Let in every home a sense of fullness be born,
Bathed in light, like the break of dawn,
Let love resonate in every brick and every wall,
A sanctuary of solace, where kindness is the call.

From the love's soil, let buds of prosperity sprout,
In this land of hope, let all souls be devout.
As the fragrance of abundance fills the air,
May it be a gift for everyone to share.

Lord, banish hate and revenge from the human heart,
Let tenderness find its voice in our works of art,
May virtue's lofty mountains with majestic might
Guard our fragile planet from the darkest of the night.

Let us strive for a world, brave and bright,
With love and compassion as the guiding light.
In this shared dream, our spirits shall be free,
To create a world of peace, for you and me.

BOOK IV

Lights of Life

The Hand

The healing hand of the Son of Man
Brings forth miracles to our land.
To awaken humanity to wisdom's light,
Its divine touch dispels the night.
The hand, a conduit for Heaven's grace,
Can infuse joy into every face.
The blind can see, the lame can stand,
Transformed by a shepherd's gentle hand.
Through stormy seas and trials steep,
It can still a tempest, calm the weep.
From water turned to wine's delight,
To feed thousands in their plight,
In every blessing, a message clear,
Of celestial compassion, ever near,
A touch, a word, a feel so grand,
It is all in this wondrous hand.
Humanity can cherish this timeless tale,
Of miracles that will never pale,
The Son of Man, divinely planned,
With sacred power in his gentle hand.

Divine Grace

(Inspired by Rabindranath Tagore)

Dear Lord our Savior, please be so kind
To grant life to the sick, and sight to the blind.
You, an ocean of love, can easily spare a drop,
To heal your children and to prop
Their souls parched by the heat of this mortal life,
As they seek your compassion in their daily strife.
Bring forth tears, from your love's gentle rain;
Fill their eyes, wash away their pain.
Gather your children, thirsty and forlorn;
Lay 'em by the stream of your love, reborn.
In your divine embrace, let their spirits thrive,
Immersed in your grace, where love shall revive.

Faith

In the sacred world to which the faithful turn,
A paradox of sight, we shall discern,
For naked eyes, being naturally confined,
Never see things as, by intuition, defined.
In realms unseen, with truth's elusive trace,
Mysteries are shrouded beyond mere space.

With his threads of doubt intertwined,
The doubting Thomas questions the divine,
Longs to see, to touch the wounds of grace,
To prove the resurrection's sacred place.
But in this tale, a message is concealed,
The faith's true essence is never revealed.

Thomas, with his hands upon the scars,
Cannot see the truth beyond the stars.
He seeks in flesh what faith alone could give,
Misses the deeper call, the truth to live,
For faith is not found in tactile things,
But only in the soul, where intuition sings.

The intuitive mind, a beacon bright,
Illumes the path with a mysterious light;
It looks beyond the veil of the physical,
And peers into the realm of the mystical.
In stillness, it discerns a hidden flow,
'Tis in the unseen, real faith does grow.

Do not be bound by a mere earthly gaze,
But cultivate the wisdom that conveys
The truth of faith, which needs no mortal proof,
For in the heart's vast depths, you see its groove.
With the eyes of your soul, you will find
A rich world out there even for the blind.

Ocean of Life

In life's vast ocean, our vessels we propel
Upon the boundless waves, as the Fates compel,
Each day a fleeting wave, a moment's rise and fall,
As we sail on, we may also heed the siren call.
The tides of time, the eternal ebb and flow,
We navigate the currents, both high and low.
Our choices, like ripples, spread far and wide,
Waves of consequence, on this timeless tide.
Storms may rage upon us, often at length;
Yet, within our souls, we find the strength,
To weather every squall, to steer a steady course,
In the tumultuous waters with an endless source.
The horizon beckons, a distant, hazy line,
Dreams and aspirations, like distant islands, shine.
Oh brave heart, the captain of your own design,
Navigate life's ocean, with a spirit divine,
In boundless waves, seek courage, wisdom's stealth,
Amidst the challenge, nurture your inner wealth.

Sail on

In the recess of your heart where sorrows lie,
You seek the elusive peace, a helpless cry,
But it's not in calm seas or skies of blue,
True serenity emerges from the battle in view.
The battle rages within, the sages proclaim,
Where grit and discipline fan the flame.
To conquer thyself, the daily strife you must wage,
In the tempest of your mind, on wisdom's stage.

Like a ship on stormy seas, you set your course,
With goals and plans, your driving force,
Obstacles, like towering waves, may block your way,
Yet relentlessly you sail through night and day.
In the course of time, you forge your might,
As dreams and ambitions guide your fight.
Detractors, like gusty winds, may taunt and jeer,
But you sail on, undeterred, with a vision clear.

Success, a distant star, you strive to reach,
Through the raging tempest you dare to breach.
With unwavering resolve, you steer your fate,
Through the darkest night, you illuminate.
The rhythm of your efforts, a steady drumbeat,
In the face of adversity, you find your feat,
For it's in the throes of challenges that you see
The essence of your soul, the truth of your decree.

Author

In life's grand play, you wield the quill,
The author of your life, with boundless skill.
Don't fear the ink, don't hesitate, but rewrite,
Craft your narrative, in the darkest night.

Unfold your pages, let authenticity shine,
A canvas vast, your essence, your design.
Break free from chains, from herds that roam,
For only then your true self will find a home.

In a world of echoes, where norms dictate,
Your voice, your vision, don't underestimate.
Let your colors blend, in a palette unique,
In your artistry, the answers you shall seek.

Fear not the void, nor the unknown trail,
Embrace your essence, let your spirit sail.
On the stage of existence, play your part,
Craft meanings from the depths of your heart.

Since life's true purpose lies in your hand,
To mold, to shape, to make a stand,
As the author of your tale, bold and free,
Lend meanings to life in the script's decree.

Confessions of Dr. Faust

In this solemn stance, burdened and bound,
Weight of choices, darkness profound.
As I reflect, I am compelled to confess,
My desires' depths, consequences, and distress.
In my thirst for power, deception I embraced,
Made a pact with the devil, my soul I disgraced.
Claimed by forbidden realms, lost in the maze,
Stung by remorse, now I stand in a daze.
Pleasures I sought, brief satisfaction in tow,
Yet guilt's mark I carry on conscience's flow.
To atone for transgressions, with honesty's face,
I seek forgiveness; oh! let me attain my soul's grace.
Oh Destiny, from your chains, how I long to be free,
To seek salvation, break away, and find liberty.

The Sacred Prophecy

In his premonition, a tyrant's dreadful dream,
The king sought to thwart the prophecy, it seemed,
To defend his throne, he pronounced doom,
A massacre, where he claimed the innocent's tomb.
But Fate, with skeins of purpose intertwined,
Would not let darkness veil the light divine.
Despite a king's decree that sought to erase,
The Son of Man would emerge in humble grace.

Through the pall of gloom in Bethlehem's night,
A greater truth would shine gentle and bright—
The power of kings, a fleeting gleam,
Cannot darken a providential dream.
From Bethlehem's despair, as history learned,
Atrocity and power would humbly be overturned.
A child would grow, a beacon in the mire,
With his teachings to lead humanity higher.

As Destiny, aligned with the divine decree,
Revealed her plan, we are all meant to see,
In the darkest hours, the light would find its way,
In the heart of man, a brighter realm would sway.
In the tragic tale of Bethlehem's night,
Where tyranny clashed with eternal light,
The prophecy was fulfilled, the message profound,
A new king to be hailed, and humanity unbound.

Stairway to Heaven

Upon these steps of virtue's stone,
A stairway to Heaven brightly shown.
The divine covenant eternally true,
Guiding us upwards, to the skies of blue.
Surmounting challenges, with courage anew,
Each righteous act, a step we pursue,
It all gleams in every riser,
A stairway to Heaven not for a miser.
Wisdom's rocks hewn, the foundation strong,
Empathy's blocks, we carry along,
Forgiveness and love, the mortar we bind,
Ascent to the divine, in each virtuous mind.
It's the compassion's handrail that we grip,
As we journey upwards, on our paradise trip.
Humility's essence, each stone we carve,
On the stairway to Heaven, souls never starve.
On harmony's path, each soul ascends,
On steps of bliss, joy never ends,
As we all forge ahead, stones of virtue we hone,
A stairway to Heaven, in hearts, brightly shown.

Oh Judas

Oh Judas, tell us now,
what vile intent did you possess,
To betray the Son of Man,
In the darkness, to transgress?
What thoughts did brew,
Within your twisted heart,
To tear apart a bond of love,
And play a traitor's part?

Oh Judas, tell us now,
Was it worth the price you paid,
To be forever marked by infamy,
By the choices that you made?
What devious corners of the soul
Drove you to a mortal sin?
To betray a friend, a brother,
And let darkness reign within?

Deceptive whispers in your ear,
A cunning, sinister voice,
Did they drown out the wisdom,
The teachings, the righteous choice?
What motives spurred you on,
To hang a righteous man,
Upon a cross of suffering,
To fulfill a wicked plan?

Since man's nature can be cruel,
An eternal, smoldering spark,
A struggle between good and evil,
A subtle blend of light and dark.
Judas, your act serves a lesson,
A symbol of betrayal's art,
A tale of basest instincts
That lie in all our hearts.

The Battle Within

In the fortress of your mind, you craft your fate,
A treacherous realm where doubts and fears await
Their daily battle, an internal strife,
An epic quest to sculpt a vibrant life.
But once you conquer doubts that lie inside,
External skepticism will no longer deride.
In the sanctum of self-belief, discover your might,
Let others' opinions fade in the empowering light.
To thrive, to chase dreams, and to prevail,
Unleash the power within, unfurl the sail,
Steer the voyage with unbridled force,
Transform your thoughts to guide the course.
As clarity dawns, with your strength profound,
You silence the doubts with an imperious sound.
An architect of fate with your own decree,
You empower your soul, set your spirit free.

Dedication

In dreams of glory, where stars softly gleam,
Success is but a distant, elusive theme.
It's not the faint-hearted who claim the prize,
But those with a fire in their determined eyes.

Relentless dedication, the path they tread,
Where many falter, they forge ahead.
With genuine labor, their steadfast guide,
They make their ambitions life's only stride.

Obsession and drive, their constant friend,
They chase their dreams to no foreseeable end.
To strangers, their passion may seem insane,
Yet that sets them apart from the mundane.

They stand resilient, in the face of despair,
Stoic strength, their shield, a garment they wear.
They march through storms, both fierce and mild,
Their unyielding spirit, a testament, undefiled.

Obstacles and challenges, they welcome with grace,
For in overcoming, they find their rightful place.
Success, they understand, isn't given, it's earned,
Through a commitment unbroken, a passion unburned.

Such are the souls, the beacon of light,
For those in pursuit, day and night,
To remind us all, in our quest for the great,
Dedication and hard work determine our fate.

God is Dead, Nietzsche is Not

"Is there no God?" A question to explore,
The purpose of life we ought to restore,
Since without God in his age-old guise,
'Tis a shocking perception our belief defies.
We're thrust into a world that is unknown,
Where the essence of man is to be sown.
No more sheltered by celestial might,
We carve a world to see the light,
To shape our destiny, to forge our way,
To weave our narratives, to make our day.
In the absence of God, we behold
Man's true self, sacred and old.
To ponder morality, and what's right,
For Love and wisdom must shed light
On our existence; through introspection
We cultivate our own reflection,
To answer the question, as our hearts have bled,
How to find life after "God is dead."

A Fakir and His Idol

In a realm ruled by edicts stern and bold,
No idolatry allowed, as the tale unfolds.
A poor fakir, illiterate, unaware,
Sat at the park, with his idols laid bare.
With flowers and lamps, his offerings grand,
He sought alms from the passers'-by hands.
Since he didn't know of the ruler's decree,
He carried on, just as carefree.

But soldiers came, their duty to uphold,
One seized his collar, steadfast and bold.
With a cruel look, they crushed his art,
Under their boots, they broke it apart.
His idol shattered, a heart-wrenching sight,
The fakir, torn apart, like day turning to night.
Tearful eyes gazed upon the debris,
An innocent victim, oh, why must it be?

Oblivious of the edict's dire decree,
A poor fakir and a world he couldn't see.
A tale of loss, of innocence denied,
In the shadows of power, humanity cried.
In this realm of rules and ruthless might,
Compassion's call was nowhere in sight.
As justice's weight was pressed tight,
The less one had, the heavier the burden's bite.

Creation of Adam

In this divine tableau, a truth unfolds,
A testament to what our hearts behold,
That in his quest for knowledge and truth,
He seeks a higher purpose, an ageless youth.

The hands, a bridge between earth and sky,
A symbol of mankind's ceaseless quest to fly,
To touch the heavens, know the depths within,
To fathom mysteries, and to shed its sin.

Since in humans' very forms, the divine theme,
The lights of God, in their souls, gently beam,
Each human soul is a masterpiece of art,
A microcosm of a divine, cosmic chart.

As they reach for wisdom's distant shore,
On a spiritual quest, they seek out forevermore,
Infinite potential in their finite frames,
Within this paradox, they stake their claims.

Oh, Michelangelo, your brush did tell,
The tale of mankind, bound by a mortal shell,
Yet reaching for the heavens, ever near,
A testament to what it means to be here.

In "Creation of Adam," we find our creed,
A call to rise, to love, to intercede,
To celebrate our earthly, mortal desires,
And in our quest, find meanings in the fire.

Awakening to Oneness

Let our hearts, in compassion, intertwine,
Let understanding be our guiding sign.
With empathy, we'll feel others' plight,
And shed prejudices that often blind our sight.
Proud of others' success, others' joys we'll share,
Weep for their woes, their burdens we'll bear.
The rainbow's hues, we'll marvel the same,
Skin color irrelevant, no judgment to tame.
The ocean's embrace, for all, it shall be,
Cultures woven together, harmoniously.
Majestic mountains, equal in their awe,
Regardless of a mansion or humble straw.
In hymns to the cherubs, our voices align,
Religion's shadow, we shall leave behind.
Paradise on earth, a world we'll create,
Harmonious, beautiful, as dreams dictate.
Together we'll forge, with strength unfurled,
A better realm for all, a gift to the world.

Doubt the Doubters!

In the hall of critique, we find our forge,
Where negativity's flames may burn and scorch.
Detractors, like fire, can consume our doubt,
Yet from their embers, resolve will sprout.

Behold, when they speak in tongues of scorn,
It is only then our hidden strengths are born.
In their whispers, in their bitter game,
Lies the fuel that sustains our inner flame.

Our goals, like precious metals, must be refined,
In the furnace of doubt, they're redefined.
We are the alchemists of our fate,
Transforming adversity into gold innate.

Embrace your uniqueness, be a blazing star,
Let the critics' clamor be heard from afar.
Their noise, like distant thunder, shall fade,
As you chart your course, unfazed, unafraid.

In this drama of life's grand scheme,
Let detractors be the fire of your dream.
Forge your destiny with ruthless power,
Amidst the shadows, stand like a tower.

Resolve

Within the walls of the mind, two voices dwell,
One speaks softly, in comfort's soothing spell,
"Stay in the warmth of ease, don't strive or strain,
Embrace the gentle lull, release your grasp on pain."

Yet in the depths, another voice takes root and grows,
It challenges our essence, the path it boldly shows,
"Consider what could bloom, if you but dare to try,
Toil with a purpose and reach for heights in the sky."

The latter, a beacon burning with relentless fire,
Guides us through the tempest, ignites our desire.
It calls for excellence, and diligence its creed,
Even when an easier road tempts us with greed.

Since success is a reward not easily earned,
But through sweat and tears, in lessons learned.
In the crucible of struggles, our strengths are honed,
We forge the very tools that etch our names in stone.

When the path grows steep, and hardships cloud our way,
Remember, we must endure, persist, and never sway.
Life is a game of wits; we must master its grand design,
To live without regret, our aspirations we must align.

Social Acceptance

To fit in with the crowd, a mask we wear,
A persona that is outwardly fair.
To face the world, we don this guise,
A social script, that truth defies.
A mask of smiles, or stoic grace,
Conforming to our time and place,
The persona serves a vital role
In navigating our society's scroll.
But deep within, a mystery dwells,
Unseen until our life compels;
Since dangers lurk in our core,
The self within, we must explore.
In careful reflection, we find the key,
To unlock the soul and set it free.

Be Yourself

From dogma's bonds set yourself free.
Cast off the chains of societal decree.
Question the norms, the status quo.
Dare to wander where others fear to go.
In the depths of your soul, a flame burns bright.
Bring it out, and prepare to fight
Those who try to rein you in.
Show them your courage, your power within.

Hold your passions, your desires untamed,
Let them soar and dance, unashamed.
Unveil the masks that you always wear;
Embrace your flaws, for they make you rare.
But with great power, there comes great weight,
Responsibility for the choices you'll create.
Own your triumphs, your defeats as well,
For it is through both, that you truly excel.

Maya

In life's vast tapestry, we weave our threads,
Ceaselessly through moments, as Destiny treads.
To connect to each strand, a purpose we find,
Yet in Maya's honey trap, we often lose our minds.
Maya's veils shimmer, a beguiling mirage,
Worldly attachments, her tempting entourage.
As we yield to her, for ephemeral gain,
Our true essence, we sadly restrain.

Mortal life's purpose, in this cosmic play,
Is not mere indulgence in what soon shall decay.
It's a journey of the spirit, a quest for the divine,
To connect with the eternal, in every fleeting sign.
Detach from the chains of desire's endless plea,
Seek the inner sanctum where truth and light be.
In the temple of the self, the soul's silent prayer,
Find liberation from Maya's transient snare.

Connect to the world with love and grace,
But let not attachments define your space.
In the pursuit of spirit, let your heart be free,
For in detachment, the true fulfillment shall be.
In the symphony of existence, let your soul be the song,
Unattached, undistracted, where you truly belong.
Ascend the spiritual summit where illusions depart,
And in the oneness of all, find the essence of your heart.

Ego

(Inspired by Rabindranath Tagore)

Under the veil of night, I embark on a quest,
To meet Thee, my Lord, and to be blessed.
Yet, a chilling presence follows me, unseen—
A shadowy figure, too eerie and too keen.
I take a sudden turn just to elude
The strange ghost, so nagging and so crude.
Relief washes over me, as I catch my breath,
But soon that eerie feeling returns, like death.

In a sudden awakening, clarity does strike.
I do recognize the shadow that I fiercely dislike.
A character too familiar, hubristic, and loud—
It's my dreadful Ego, always seeking to crowd.
Whether awake or asleep, he lingers near,
Stomping and romping fills me with fear.
He trumps me and jabs me at every chance,
Silencing my voice, thus leaving me in a trance.

How can I approach Thy divine gate, my Lord,
Tethered to such company as if with a cord?
Help me, Lord, to shed this Ego's chain,
So that I stand before Thee, free from disdain.

Time the Jester

> No man ever steps in the same river twice, for it's not the same river and he's not the same man.
> —Heraclitus

On life's grand stage, time jests,
Laughing at our endeavors, transient quests.
Remember, a philosopher once did decree,
No man steps in a river twice, as we see.

Nature whispers truth, a cyclical rhyme,
Flowers bloom, then fade, with passing time.
Butterflies emerge, beauty's brief delight,
Ephemeral beings, a fleeting sight.

Great emperors and warriors renowned,
Now reduced to dust in history's ground.
Celestial stars, they shine so bright,
Yet mortal fate, they can't fight.

Time mocks our ego's stardom,
Triumph and defeat, senses' freedom.
In folly, we forget the eternal dance,
Swayed by emotions with a fleeting chance.

Change of Wheels

I strutted with pride, a giant's ego reigned,
The road my sovereignty, my temper unchained,
Road rage a daily affair, I'd provoke a senseless fight,
Little did I know destiny would soon set things right.

A crash, a devastating shattering of all I knew,
In one fateful moment, my journey was set askew—
Sat in a wheelchair, I navigated a new aisle,
Paid humbly for the cost of an arrogant style.

Still in the stillness, a transformation began,
I glimpsed the truths and grandeur of the plan.
Humility's silk, a new robe now I wear,
And a noble vista, an exalted world I share.

Empathy's light gently warms my heart,
Replacing the anger that once tore me apart.
Compassion blooms like a flower within my soul,
In others' struggles, now I find a common goal.

Kindness like a balm heals wounds so deep,
Relieves the burdens that I always used to keep.
I've learned the power of letting go of disdain,
As forgiveness dispels the most harrowing of pain.

Oh Fate, the wheels of my car were once my pride,
Now, the wheels of this chair, humility my guide.
No longer trapped in pride and ego's snare,
Maimed and disabled, yet I've got love to spare.

Your Higher Self

To find true peace within yourself,
Into a deeper root, you ought to delve.
Release the ego, let the spirit rise,
To the higher self, where harmony lies.
In humble surrender, set your burdens free,
In the soul's whispers, the essence to see.
No longer bound by earthly desires,
In the realm of serenity, the heart inspires.
Unveil the truth through inner reflection,
The higher self's wisdom, a divine connection.
Surrender, dear soul, to your inner light,
Discover the peace, shining ever bright.
Let your higher self lead you with gentle sway,
In its loving decree, find solace every day.

The Universe Within

> To see a World in a Grain of Sand
> And a Heaven in a Wild Flower,
> Hold Infinity in the palm of your hand
> And Eternity in an hour . . .
>
> —WILLIAM BLAKE, Auguries of Innocence

In the crystal chalice of my mortal frame,
Gathers the universe, no two drops the same.
From the ocean's depth, where mysteries hide,
To the river's flow, in ceaseless ebb and tide,
The raindrops' fall from the heavens' weep,
A cycle eternal that nature's secrets keep,
From distant clouds, where thunderstorms brew,
Each droplet whispers tales both old and new.

As water I drink bears Earth's liquid grace,
My very being holds a cosmic trace.
Stardust particles in my flesh intertwine,
A dance of atoms in the very form of mine.
Within, the soul, a spark of divine light,
A beacon burning, ever shining bright.
But ego's cloak, a heavy shroud I wear,
Enchanted by Maya, life's truth I fail to bear.

In this illusion, I stumble, and I fall,
Forgetting the unity that embraces all.
Oh my foolish heart, shed this ego's guise,
See the grand stage, where every soul sighs.
Rise and walk with hearts and minds free,
And grasp the oneness, the cosmic tapestry,
In drops and stardust where spirits intertwine,
The universe within, our souls divine.

Fetus

In the womb's cocoon, a cosmic enigma in slumber,
A mystery unfurling, revealing a divine wonder,
From the tiniest cell, a soul is in flight,
A dance of creation, through day and night.
Oh Fetus, most wondrous in the universe's span,
A nature's riddle, crafted by a master plan,
From stardust to heartbeat, from silence to song,
A journey of magic, where we all belong.

In a sacred cradle, life's secrets interlace,
A confluence of beginnings, in a miracle's embrace,
Thoughts bloom like flowers, synapses intertwine,
A network of neurons, and a mind begins to shine.
Love courses through veins like ripples of light,
Invisible dreams are woven in the depth of night.
From the blueprint of cells, a life begins its fight,
A metamorphosis of being, from darkness to light.

Oh, the perpetual heartbeat, the will to survive,
In the fetal dreamscape, you learn how to thrive.
From the mysteries of galaxies to Earth's embrace,
You whisper truths of the human race.
With a new heart that is just about to thrum,
From one cell's whisper to the beating of a drum,
Fetus, you're the poetry, the universe's art,
A testament to life's unrelenting, resilient heart.

Resilience

On the shore of time where we stand,
Trials and tribulations test our hand.
Resilience, a beacon in the darkest hour,
Does guide us all with relentless power.

As life's storms strike, without remorse,
And doubts and fears take their course,
We stand firm, and our essence shines,
For it's in adversity, we redefine our lines.

The external world may twist and sway,
But our resilience will light the way.
With composure, we face the tempest's roar,
Finding solutions on this unknown shore.

We take responsibility for our destiny's call,
No longer victims but masters of all.
Pain becomes the fuel that drives our quest,
To reach new heights, we'll give our best.

As we steer through the darkness, as we ascend,
In the quest for our purpose, we break and mend.
Success, we must crave it like the air we breathe,
Unbroken and undefeated, we rise from beneath.

Life

On an unknown path, we start our quest,
Each step a painting in the world's grand bequest.
A work of art, we paint with passion and strife,
With colors of love and moments of life.

On the pages of time, we pen our own story,
A book we write, filled with guilt and glory.
With chapters of triumph and hardships we brave,
We script our destiny in life's eternal wave.

Life is a song, a melody that we compose,
With verses of joy and sorrow, and our prose.
The music of our time, a cosmic symphony so grand,
We dance to its rhythm in a vast, mysterious land.

A game of chance, with rules and choices to make,
We strategize, we play, we bend but do not break.
In a world of mayhem, where challenges collide,
Life is a game, an odyssey deep and wide.

Yet above all, life is a gift, a treasure divine,
A present unwrapped, with love's tender sign.
In its fragile moments, we find our purpose and shift,
Discover in this earthly journey a unique gift.

Delight in this journey, the art, the song,
Dance through its pages and play along.
Embrace the challenge, and let your spirit lift,
For in every facet of life, you hold a precious gift.

Gratitude

Shall we stand with gratitude in heart,
A few words that we ought to impart,
With each sunrise, a thankful start,
Appreciating the universe's work of art.
In moments of triumph and lessons learned,
In challenges faced, where growth is earned,
For the kindness of strangers, a helping hand,
Or the wisdom of the sages, let us understand—
Storms may rage, skies may be gray,
Still our gratitude, with us, will stay,
For the good and the bad, woven in strife,
Richness in both, shaping our life.

Blessings

(Inspired by Rabindranath Tagore)

There are deaths and tragedies, agonies and pains.
Life still brings us joy, love, and blissful gains.
The sun still bathes us in golden light.
The moon still greets us in the quiet night.
Gentle breezes bring secrets to share,
Caressing trees with tender care.
The ocean's dance with its waves in tune,
A rhythm of life under the radiant moon.
Life's vast expanse, boundless and free,
Stretching to infinity, for all to see.
Dear Lord, let me offer my plea,
For this gift of life, I bow to Thee.
Let me savor its honey with endless delight,
A celebration of love, from morn to night.

United through Him

In the vast expanse of cosmic wonder,
    Where galaxies swirl and stars ignite,
It's a truth, profound and tender,
    A timeless essence, pure and bright,
Whispering through the rustling leaves,
    And rippling across the tranquil seas,
The melody of life in a splendid weave,
    His presence here to infinite degrees.

In every breath, a shared connection,
    Threads of life entwined tight,
Divine love, a deep reflection,
    Uniting souls in eternal light.
We are drops in an ocean,
    Individual yet part of the His design,
Each one a unique notion,
    Still united in the family divine.

Since He is the sacred bond,
    That unites us in our earthly quest,
To His love, we must respond,
    To the call of unity, at His behest.

The Sacred Tongue

Ramakrishna's tongue, nature's gift divine,
A wellspring of wisdom, sweeter than wine,
Endowed with magic, the tongue did hold
Secrets of the cosmos, as mysteries unfold.
In the land of knowledge, a mighty tree,
With branches of truth to set us free,
Roots in Heaven, in hallowed ground,
Leaves of wisdom, rustling with a mystic sound.
Each syllable it uttered, in a spell of trance,
Narrating tales from life's eternal dance,
Like a magician's incantation, it conjured the sublime,
Enlightening thoughts, transcending space and time.
In its words, we found solace, transcendental peace,
Treasures of wisdom that never seemed to cease.
A beacon in the dark, a guide through the night,
The sacred tongue has given us the light.
With its teachings, we trace our way back home,
To the heart of existence, under a divine dome.

Shiva's Dance

On the cosmic stage, emerging from the night,
    Where creation and destruction intertwine,
In rhythms divine, in the eternal light,
    Shiva's dance, the Creation's grand design.

With His grace, the stage is set,
    For Shiva to cavort with a thunderous sound,
The world awakens, as lights are met,
    In His tandava dance, mysteries unbound.

With fiery gaze and third eye's sight,
    He spins the tale of life's grand stance,
Creation bursts forth, a divine light,
    From his locks, the Ganges springs to dance.

Yet in the circle of sacred blaze,
    Destruction's rhythm begins to play,
For every dawn must yield to dusk's haze,
    And galaxies, to stardust, must decay.

With Shiva's tandava, worlds dissolve,
    In sacred flames, they find their end,
Yet from the ashes, new lives evolve,
    The cosmic cycle, ever to ascend.

In endless cycles, the dance goes on,
    Creation's splendor, destruction's bane,
An ebb and flow, through dusk and dawn,
    A dance eternal, no end, no chain.

Death

Is Death an eternal slumber we endure,
Or a passage to realms unseen, obscure?
Do we fade like stars, swallowed by night,
Or ascend to realms bathed in ethereal light?

A transition, not an end, as some may perceive,
In life's cosmic dance, where worlds interweave.
Still, as day surrenders to the embrace of night,
Mortality's cycle completes, in Death's somber light.

Our fate seems sealed at the moment of birth,
In Death's gentle whisper, to return to earth.
The fleeting life is like nature's dance,
From dust we rise, to dust we advance.

Death, the quiet companion, to life's parade,
A truth that consciously we often evade,
Yet it shapes our existence, gives meaning to be,
In its shadow, we gaze upon the eternity's sea.

Philosophers offer perspectives diverse,
On death's enigma, each view a unique verse,
From existential questions to spiritual quests,
Death is still a riddle in a philosophy fest.

A Divine Encounter

My mortal body lay still, unconscious and frail,
I soared beyond the confines, my essence set sail.
It's a different plane, where reality seemed to cease,
A breathtaking journey, to a world of boundless peace.
A realm of luminescence, pain dissolved like dew,
A sense of weightlessness, as I gently flew.
With no earthly burdens tethering me down,
Just boundless love my spirit did surround.

A river of knowledge flowed through my core,
Mysteries and truths, I had never known before,
A sense of understanding, without words or speech,
The secrets of the universe, it seemed to teach.
Time loses its meaning in this ethereal place,
Past, present, and future, merging in space,
A state of being, free from earthly strife,
Where conflicts lose their meaning in life.

In a flash, my earthly life unfolded like a cosmic scroll,
I sensed every joy and every pain that took its toll.
Suddenly, a divine voice echoed through the light,
As I was deeply immersed in this ethereal flight—
"Your journey's not over, you must return,
To the earthly realm, where lessons you'll learn,
Your purpose is incomplete, your story's not done,
Go back with love, for you are a chosen one."

The Train of Destiny

(Dedicated to all victims of Coromandel Express accident in India on June 2nd, 2023)

La—LaLaLa—La—LaLaLa!

Months of joy, my heart did thrum,
To Chennai and the holy temples, I'd come.
For years, God's call, a beckoning voice,
Drawing me near and urging my choice.

Chug-Chug . . . Chug-Chug!

On board with my wife, bright and breezy,
With snacks and tea, taking it easy.
A young girl, aged seven or eight,
Nagged her mom to be her playmate.
Inside the carriage, a rhythm of life,
With wheels churning, there's no strife.
All seemed jolly, with spirits high,
Bound for destinations, far and nigh.

Bang, the big bang, bigger than the big bang!

A thunderous jolt, like lightning's flare,
In an instant, darkness choked all the air.
Intense pain shattered my frame,
I felt nothing, engulfed by a flame.

Sinking, descending, a black hole grasped,
Oh God, where are you? I gasped.
Wasn't I on my sacred quest?
To pay my homage, to be blessed?

Yikes, Holy Smoke!

Baffled and bewildered, I stand in a daze.
What's going on? I'm lost in a haze.
No pain to my senses, weightless and free,
Afloat like a feather, oh, what could it be?
I gaze upon myself, a contorted figure,
Soaked in blood, to move he's not eager.
Through metal walls, I glide with ease,
A realm unknown, oh God, help me please.

Aaaaaaaaaaaaaa!

Screams fill the air, piercing through the night,
Distraught voices wail, agony at its height.
A cacophony of pleas, desperate and dire,
Cries of anguish, consumed by fire.
Mangled carriages strewn, twisted, and torn,
Disfigured bodies scattered, a scene forlorn.
Oh God, where are You in this abyss of despair?
Why this horror? This burden, how can we bear?

Shhhhhhhhhhhhh!

Unawares, now I float, well above the plain,
Where twinkling lights in darkness wane.
A realm of peace, where attachments cease,
In this ethereal grace, a sense of release.
A bright white light draws near, ever more bright,
It pulls me with a charm, some soothing might.
Compelled to follow, my path unclear,
To an unknown destination, I now adhere.
A voice whispers, promising a divine affair,
A tryst with God, awaiting me there.
In exclamation, I scream and impart,
"Oh God, how great Thou art!" from my heart.

Urn of Ashes

Upon the urn I let my thoughtful gaze rest,
Moments frozen, a revelation blessed—
Not a vessel of sorrow, but a celebration of life,
Every chapter, every moment, from joy to strife,
In the ashes!

Childhood's laughter, like sunlight's gleam,
Woven with hopes, like a cherished dream,
Adventures started with fearless might,
Each grain of memory, shining so bright,
In the ashes!

From innocence's look to wisdom's gaze,
The passage of time, in subtle ways,
A tapestry woven of joys and tears,
Stored within the urn, for so many years,
In the ashes!

The first blush of love, so tender, so sweet,
A young heart that would forever beat,
Romance's whispers, like a gentle breeze,
All captured within, as time does freeze,
In the ashes!

And oh, the tales of a heart that broke,
A sigh and tears it would quietly evoke,
Lessons learned, redemption of life's art,
Emotions' mosaic, etched in every part,
In the ashes!

Let the urn stand as an emblem sublime,
Let the bells of life eternally chime,
For it's an urn of tales, not of death,
A joyous celebration of every breath,
In the ashes!

On the Shore of Eternity

My life may fade in the twilight's glow,
Fear not, my love, for I shall return, you'll know.
I am an eternal soul, I will not forever depart,
When I'm not here do not grieve, my sweetheart.

Winter's frost steals warmth, and days grow cold,
Yet, it heralds a tale of rebirth, age-old and bold;
So too does Death's veil, a cosmic, mystic thing,
Preparing the grand stage for a new life to sing.

Born again in realms unknown, I shall arise,
In a different world, under different skies,
New parents and new siblings to embrace,
A child reborn with love's tender grace.

Perhaps, in life's labyrinth, we'll cross once more,
Yet, you won't recognize the soul you knew before.
Once more I'll dance with butterflies in flight,
And build castles in the sand in pure delight.

Rainbows shall arch over my wandering soul,
I'll drink the rain, as life's stories unfold.
Perhaps on a wall, I'll etch a new name,
Yet the essence within remains the same.

How splendid is the dance of life's refrain,
A celebration unending, free from Death's chain!
In each rebirth, a chance to learn and grow,
A cosmic ocean where forever we shall flow.

The End

www.ingramcontent.com/pod-product-compliance
Lightning Source LLC
Chambersburg PA
CBHW060522090426
42735CB00011B/2336